ST GREGORY OF NAZIANZUS

On God and Man

T0355689

ST VLADIMIR'S SEMINARY PRESS
Popular Patristics Series
Number 21

The Popular Patristics Series published by St Vladimir's Seminary Press provides readable and accurate translations of a wide range of early Christian literature to a wide audience—students of Christian history to lay Christians reading for spiritual benefit. Recognized scholars in their fields provide short but comprehensive and clear introductions to the material. The texts include classics of Christian literature, thematic volumes, collections of homilies, letters on spiritual counsel, and poetical works from a variety of geographical contexts and historical backgrounds. The mission of the series is to mine the riches of the early Church and to make these treasures available to all.

Series Editor
BOGDAN BUCUR

Associate Editor
IGNATIUS GREEN

* * *

Series Editor
1999–2020
JOHN BEHR

On God and Man

THE THEOLOGICAL POETRY OF
ST GREGORY OF NAZIANZUS

Translated and Introduced by
PETER GILBERT

ST VLADIMIR'S SEMINARY PRESS

YONKERS, NEW YORK

Library of Congress Cataloging-in-Publication Data

Gregory, of Nazianzus, Saint.
    On God and man: the theological poetry of St Gregory of Nazianzus / translated
and introduced by Peter Gilbert.
        p. cm.
    Includes bibliographical references (p.).
    ISBN 0–88141–220–1 (alk. paper)
    1. Gregory, of Nazianzus, Saint—Translations into English. 2. Christian
poetry, Greek—Translations into English. 3. Theology—Poetry. I. Gilbert, Peter
(Peter L.) II. Title.

    PA3998.G73 A235 2001
    881'.01—dc21

                                                              2001034911

COPYRIGHT © 2001 BY
ST VLADIMIR'S SEMINARY PRESS
575 Scarsdale Road, Yonkers, NY 10707
1-800-204-2665
www.svspress.com

ISBN 0–88141–220–1
ISSN 1555–5755

PRINTED IN THE UNITED STATES OF AMERICA

In memory of my mother

Contents

Acknowledgements

Acknowledgements are due to Professor Robin Darling Young, of the Catholic University of America, who first introduced me to St Gregory's poetry and under whose supervision the dissertation was written for which most of these poems were originally translated; to my editor, Dr John Behr, of St Vladimir's Seminary, for his patience and perseverance; and to my uncle and aunt, George and Mary Sioras, of Brookline, Massachusetts, who housed me during most of the time that these translations were being prepared. To all the above, Many Years.

Introduction

At the end of his life, after resigning his position as archbishop of Constantinople in the midst of the Second Ecumenical Council and returning to his native Cappadocia, St Gregory of Nazianzus (known as "the Theologian") retired to a secluded life at home in an obscure, muddy village, and wrote poetry. His practice of writing poetry did not begin in these final years of his life (381–390); however, it is almost certain that most of his poetry that we possess dates from this time. And there is quite a lot of it: about 19,000 lines, occupying most of two volumes of Migne's *Patrology*. The present volume presents a small portion of this vast literary production in English translation. There are numerous reasons why one might wish to read Gregory's poems, and numerous aspects one might consider in them—literary, historical, doctrinal, devotional. The purpose of the present Introduction is to relate, very briefly, something about Gregory the man, the poet, and the theologian, about the content and form of the poems here translated, and their literary worth, and also, if possible, to state wherein the unity of the poetry consists, to suggest how Gregory's poetry might tie together his thought and experience.

Gregory of Nazianzus is one of the great writers and luminaries of the early Church; he is traditionally venerated as one of the Three Great Hierarchs, along with Basil of Caesarea and John Chrysostom. In his case, the term "luminary" takes on a special appropriateness. Gregory was convinced that man is a light, an image and effulgence of that highest Light that is God. His writing is not only filled with images of light, as will become abundantly clear to the reader of these poems, but, as in icon painting where the light that illumines the figures seems to shine not from outside them but from within,

3

so also in Gregory's writing it would be hard for a perceptive reader to miss the light that shines through his words. It is, undoubtedly, the same light spoken of by that other Theologian, the Apostle John: "That was the true Light, which illumines every man that comes into the world" (Jn 1.99). In these poems, the light of Christ comes to us through the medium of Gregory's own very human personality. This medium is not a distorting mirror. Gregory was as convinced as any man has ever been that Jesus Christ, in order to save us, had to be fully human: "That which he has not assumed has not been healed; but that which is united to his Godhead is also saved."[1] It seems somehow appropriate that Gregory, who in his old age was one of the chief defenders of the doctrine of the full humanity of Christ against Apollinarius, should at the same time have been writing these poems in which he exhibits so fully his own humanity.

For there are things in these poems that some readers may find unsettling. Indeed, one might dispute the contention that light is a defining characteristic of Gregory's poems. Certain passages in this volume may appear distinctly bleak. Gregory seems, in some of these poems, to be struggling with what, in modern terms, might be diagnosed as a state of clinical depression: he speaks of going about under a black cloud (poem 1.2.14, 22), of assaults of demons (poem 1.2.14, 101; poem 2.1.21), of a loss of a sense of God's presence (poem 2.1.45, 8), of self-doubt and doubts as to the value of life (poem 1.2.15). Gregory in fact tells us that one of his chief reasons for writing poetry is that it acts for him as a kind of painkiller, in times of physical or mental suffering (see, for example, poem 1.2.14, 3–4; poem 2.1.39, 54–57). So that, if it is indeed the light of Christ that is visible in these poems, one must add that it is often perceived as a light that "shines in darkness"—yet which the darkness could not overcome. Such struggles with depression (if that is, in fact, what these poems exhibit) do not diminish the poems' value for a Christian reader; if anything, they only increase it.

[1]*Epistle* 101, PG 37:184a.

What is arguably most significant about Gregory's poems is that the very realistic portrayal of human life that they present is given, in them, a theological interpretation and grounding. The questions Gregory raises could not be answered by an antidepressant drug; they would remain even if, at some point, he were "feeling better." He is deeply aware that the only answer to questions of the meaning of human life can be found in "the light of the knowledge of the glory of God in the face of Jesus Christ" (2 Cor 4.6). That vision is what, in these poems, Gregory is constantly seeking.

In order to interpret the self-reflection that one finds in Gregory's poetry, therefore, it is not enough to subject them merely to a psychological analysis. One needs to know what he thought about God and man; one needs to relate his personal experience to his theology. This is, in fact, the main justification of the selection of the poems for this volume. There has been a tendency, among some scholars, to isolate certain of Gregory's poems, those in which the autobiographical note is most prominent, in order to draw attention to the peculiarly modern voice which can be heard in them; comparison is often drawn to Augustine, not without reason. But such readings, if they neglect the theological foundations of the author's thought, may lead to serious misunderstandings, both in Augustine's case and in Gregory's. If Gregory at time sounds "modern" in his poetry, it is not in spite of his theology, but because of it. It is a testimony to the clarity of his theological understanding, that he is able to describe the human predicament so well.

The poems here translated

Accordingly, the present volume contains examples both of what have come to be called Gregory's "dogmatic" poems and of his "poems about himself." This classification goes back to the early nineteenth century Benedictine editor of the poems, Dom A. B. Caillau, whose 1842 edition is reprinted in volumes 37 and 38 of the *Patrologia Graeca* published by J. P. Migne. Caillau divided the vast corpus of Gregory's poetry into two "books," *poemata theologica* and *poemata historica* (theological poems and historical poems), and further divided each of these books into two "sections," the first into *poemata dogmatica* and *poemata moralia* (dogmatic poems and moral poems), the second into *poemata de seipso* and *poemata quae spectant ad alios* (poems about himself and poems that have to do with other people). Within each of these divisions, Caillau arranged the poems according to his best estimate of their chronological order. Although his designations can sometimes appear fairly arbitrary, Caillau's division provides a ready scheme of enumerating the poems, which has become a more or less standard system of reference.[2]

In the order in which they appear in Caillau's edition, then, the poems here translated may be listed as follows (I have indicated also their length and verse form):

1) poem 1. 1.1, *De Patre*, "On the Father" (39 lines, dactylic hexameter).

2) poem 1.1.2, *De Filio*, "On the Son" (83 lines, hexameter).

3) poem 1.1.3, *De Spiritu Sancto*, "On the Holy Spirit" (93 lines, hexameter).

4) poem 1.1.4, *De mundo*, "Concerning the World" (100 lines, hexameter).

5) poem 1.1.5, *De Providentia*, "On Providence" (71 lines, hexameter).

6) poem 1.1.6, *De eodem argumento*, "On Providence (2)" (116 lines, iambic trimeter).

7) poem 1.1.7, *De substantiis mente praeditis*, "Concerning Spiritual Beings" (99 lines, hexameter).

8) poem 1.1.8, *De Anima*, "On the Soul" (129 lines, hexameter).

---

[2]I have adopted this classification system, using "poem" rather than the Latin "*carm.*" (for *carmen*, "song"). Thus, "poem 1.2.14, 1" refers to the first line of the fourteenth poem in section two (Moral Poems) of book one (Theological Poems) of Gregory's poetry—in other words, line one of the poem "On Human Nature."

9) poem 1.1.9, *De Testamentis et Adventu Christi*, "On the Two Covenants, and the Appearing of Christ" (99 + 60 lines, hexameter).

10) poem 1.1.10, *De Incarnatione, adversus Apollinarium*, "Against Apollinarius" (74 lines, trimeter)

11) poem 1.1.11, *De Christi Incarnatione*, "On the Incarnation of Christ" (16 lines, elegiac couplets).

12) poem 1.1.12, *De veris scripturae libris*, "Concerning the Genuine Books of Divine Scripture" (39 lines, mixed meters).

13) poem 1.1.37, *Alia de prospero itinere precatio*, "Another Prayer for a Safe Journey" (7 lines, hexameter).

14) poem 1.2.1, *In laudem virginitatis*, "In Praise of Virginity" (732 lines, hexameter).

15) poem 1.2.8, *Comparatio vitarum*, "A Comparison of Lives" (255 lines, trimeter).

16) poem 1.2.11, *Dialogus cum mundo*, "Conversation with the World" (12 lines, trimeter).

17) poem 1.2.12, *De naturae humanae fragilitate*, "On the Precariousness of Human Nature" (12 lines, elegiacs).

18) poem 1.2.13, *De eodem argumento*, "On the Precariousness of Human Nature" (2) (12 lines, elegiacs).

19) poem 1.2.14, *De humana natura*, "On Human Nature" (132 lines, elegiacs).

20) poem 1.2.15, *De exterioris hominis vilitate*, "On the Cheapness of the Outward Man" (164 lines, elegiacs).

21) poem 1.2.16, *De vitae itineribus*, "On Different Walks of Life" (40 lines, elegiacs).

22) poem 1.2.17, *Variorum vitae generum beatitudines*, "Blessings of Various Lives" (76 lines, elegiacs).

23) poem 1.2.18, *De vita humana*, "Concerning Human Life" (16 lines, trimeter).

24) poem 2.1.6, *Ad plebem Anastasiae*, "To His Former Congregation Anastasia" (12 lines, trimeter).

25) poem 2.1.21, *In diabolum*, "Against a Demon" (14 lines, dactylic).

26) poem 2.1.39, *In suos versus*, "On His Own Verses" (103 lines, trimeter).

27) poem 2.1.45, *De animae suae calamitatibus carmen lugubre*, "Lamentation Concerning the Sorrows of His Own Soul" (350 lines, elegiacs).

28) poem 2.1.78, *Ad suam animam*, "To His Own Soul" (17 lines, hexameter).

29) Epitaph on St Basil (6 lines, elegiacs).

Total: 2978 lines

Four kinds of poetry

These poems fall approximately into four groups. (1) The first eight poems, apart from poem 1.1.6, form a distinct series, usually referred to as the *Poemata Arcana* (poems 1.1.1–5, 7–9). They give a kind of synoptic overview or syllabus of Christian doctrine in verse, beginning with three poems treating of the mystery of the Holy Trinity, then continuing with poems upon the themes of Creation, Providence, Angels, the Human Soul, and Salvation History. The first three poems, in particular, show a considerable parallelism with Gregory's *Five Theological Orations:* if one wanted a brief, clear statement of the main ideas of these orations, shorn of technical jargon, one could hardly do better than these poems. To this first group one could add also the poem *On the Incarnation, Against Apollinarius* (poem 1.1.10), which bears a relation to Gregory's dogmatic epistle 101 (the *First Epistle to Cledonius*) similar to that which the first three *Arcana* bear to the *Five Theological Orations;* that is, it gives a brief statement, in verse form, of the longer theological work. All of these poems can be seen as a fulfillment of a promise Gregory made in his

Farewell Oration (Or. 42.26) at his departure from Constantinople in June, 381, to continue to contend for the truth with pen and ink, though no longer with his voice and in person. Finally, to this group one may add a few other doctrinal poems: another anti-Apollinarian poem (poem 1.1.11), an iambic poem *On Providence,* poem 1.1.6 (strangely placed by Caillau in the middle of the *Arcana,* though in a different meter), and a catalogue, in mixed meters, of the books of Holy Scripture recognized by Gregory as canonical (poem 1.1.12), a poem fairly often cited in histories of the Canon. All of the above, although not void of personal interest, are teaching poems, didactic verse in a strict sense; that is, the focus of the poetry is wholly on the doctrine, on what is to be believed.

(2) The poems of the second group, while not ignoring the issue of what is to be believed, are more centrally concerned with the question "What is to be done?" These, too, can be classified as teaching poems, but the personal note seems more pronounced here, though appearing in a peculiar, indirect way. That is, the issue of ethical choice, of deciding how to live one's life, is approached in these poems through the literary device of personification; the poems are framed as debates between different lives. In the long poem *In Praise of Virginity* (poem 1.2.1), after an exordium and a poetic narration of the creation of the world, the greater part of the poem consists of a formal debate between Marriage and Virginity; each gives a set speech, according to recognized rules of composition, and at the end a judgment is made, both by some unidentified judges of the contest (who may represent humanity in general) and by Christ himself. In the poem *A Comparison of Lives* (poem 1.2.8), the contestants are somewhat differently identified (the Spiritual Life and the Worldly Life), there is a single judge, and the contestants argue back and forth throughout the poem rather than speaking one after the other, but otherwise the terms and results of the debate are very similar.[3] It may be possible to give a rough dating to the poem

[3] We may note Gregory's sensitivity to poetic form: he uses heroic meter, the dactylic hexameter, in the poem that features long, formal speeches, and the meter

In Praise of Virginity; Jerome probably refers to it, and not to poem 1.2.8, when he speaks in his work *On Famous Men,* 117, of a dialogue Gregory wrote between Virginity and Marriage. Since Jerome most likely would have encountered this poem at the time when he was Gregory's student in Constantinople, in the year 380, it seems very probable that Gregory composed this poem sometime during the 370s, when he was serving as spiritual advisor to a community of nuns in Seleucia in northern Asia Minor. If this is so, then it is also likely that the poem *In Praise of Virginity* is earlier than the *Poemata Arcana,* and that the occasional identical passages between the two works[4] can be explained as Gregory reusing older material.

(3) The third grouping of poems is, in some ways, the most interesting. If the fundamental theme of the first group is what is to be believed, and that of the second group is what is to be done, the basic question of the third group seems to be "Who am I?" At least, this question is prominently raised near the beginning of a number of these poems, usually in the threefold form, "Who was I? Who am I? What am I to be?" One could describe them as philosophical meditations on human life, framed in terms of a dialogue between Gregory and his own soul. Most of these poems are written in the form of elegies, appropriate to the mood of lamentation; there are numerous echoes of other authors, from the Greek lyric poets, from the Bible (especially Job and Ecclesiastes), and from such philosophers as Heraclitus and Plato.[5] Whatever literary influences have entered into these poems' composition, they have passed through the filter of Gregory's human experience, and the result is something

of Greek drama, the iambic trimeter, in the poem in which the debate is more conversational.

[4]For instance, poem 1.117,8–12=poem 1.2.1, 15–19;poem 1.1.7, 13–16=poem 1.2.1, 31–34; poem 1.1.7, 17–19 = poem 1.2.1, 48–50; poem 1.1.8, 59–77 = poem 1.2.1, 81–99; poem 1.1.8, 80–81 = poem 1.2.1, 395–396; poem 1.1.9, 16–17 = poem 1.2.1, 131–132; poem 1.1.9, 32–40= poem 1.2.1, 137–145; poem 1.1.9,45–50=poem 1.2.1, 146–151; poem 1.1.9, 51–52=poem 1.2.1, 153–154.

[5]The contrast of human life with the life of animals at the beginning of poem 1.2.15 strongly resembles Lucretius' *De rerum natura,* V, lines 195–234, which is odd since Gregory tells us that he knew no Latin.

unique, strange, and, arguably, beautiful. (It will, perhaps, be a joy to some readers to learn that a venerable father of the Church had digestive problems and was able to complain to God about it.) While some critics have dismissed Gregory as a writer of "versified prose," and while there are, occasionally, poems of his that would support this description (poems 1.1.13–28, not translated here, are mostly versified catalogues of biblical figures and events), there seems little doubt that a piece like *On Human Nature* is a work of genuine poetry, from the hand of a genuine poet.

There are numerous short poems in this third category, some of them quite striking (e.g., poem 2.1.13, poem 2.1.78). But the most important representatives of this genre, at least among the poems translated here, are the poems *On Human Nature* and *On the Cheapness of the Outward Man* (poems 1.2.14 and 1.2.15): the two are closely connected with each other in subject matter and spirit, and give all appearance of having been written about the same time. The poem *On Human Nature,* in fact, gives precise information about where the meditation recounted in the poem took place: Gregory says that it happened the previous day, during the summer, as he was sitting in a shady grove next to a brook. Unless this is simply an allusion to Sappho or Plato's *Phaedrus* (it *is* a literary allusion, though it need not be only that), this probably means that the inspiration for the poem came to Gregory while he was sitting in the garden outside his house in Arianzus in his native Cappadocia, where he spent the last years of his life. The end of poem 1.2.15, likewise, speaks of his own death as imminent, and of priests and "wicked neighbors" who will rejoice to hear the news of this: all this corresponds pretty well with the situation of Gregory's final years. At this time, Gregory, as his biographer the priest Gregory tells us, was living at home in monastic seclusion, occupying himself in "poetic lucubrations."[6] That is, when not absorbed in prayer, he spent his nights writing verse. Such poems as *On Human Nature* and *On the Cheapness of the Outward Man* give us a kind of window onto Gregory's soul at this

---

[6]PG 35:304b.

time, allowing us to hear his internal dialogue, and to observe how, in the midst of his regrets, perplexities, and questions, he turned to God for light and hope. It is rather comforting to learn that a saint of the stature of Gregory, so often depicted on the walls of churches in timeless Byzantine majesty, went through difficulties not unlike those the rest of us face; perhaps this is one reason why the Byzantines themselves so loved to read him.

Another important poem that may reasonably be placed in this category is the *Lamentation on the Sorrows of His Own Soul* (poem 2.1.45). This, unlike the two poems just mentioned, is classified by Caillau as an autobiographical poem, but it shares with the aforesaid the same manuscript tradition; it is, like them, an elegy; and possesses much of the same spirit. Caillau seems to have judged it one of the poems of Gregory's last years, but, as Gregory speaks in this poem of his parents, who died in 374, as still living (vv. 216–226), some would date the poem to as early as 372.[7] The most memorable passage in this poem is its account of a dream Gregory had as a child, a vision of two angelic women (Chastity and Temperance), who instilled in him a longing for the angelic life (vv. 229–226. There are also interesting reflections, in the earlier of the poem, on the Pauline teaching of man's divided will.[8]

The question could be raised whether these, too, are didactic poems. One possible answer would be to say that they are not, and that this is precisely why they seem more authentically poetry. On the other hand, Gregory seems to have desired others to read his poems; if they were written for himself and God alone, why publish them? Elsewhere Gregory states, "I write for those who have had a similar experience."[9] It may be that, if these poems are meant to teach, they are meant to do so in a unique way—they are given as an act of friendship, a means of communicating person to person.

[7]Notably, Paul Gallay, *La Vie de Saint Grégoire de Nazianze* (Lyon, 1943), 253.

[8]See especially vv. 61–76, "What is this law for me?," and compare with Romans 7.

[9]Poem 2.1.1, 239ff.; see also poem 2.1.32, 50, "They are my children, as many as have drawn from me a portion of my spirit."

Gregory is aware that the question "Who am I?" about which these poems revolve is a universal human question, perhaps, the question that most needs to be asked if one is to think theologically at all; he gives these poems to lead others to ask this question for themselves.[10] In other words, while seemingly focused upon Gregory and his soul, the poems may serve a hidden evangelical function: they are meant to lead the reader to self-examination and awaken a love of God.

(4) A fourth category might be carved out for the poem *On His Own Verses* (poem 2.1.39). Caillau rightly places it among the autobiographical poems; but it is autobiographical with a difference. It is, in fact, a piece of writing about writing, a work of literary theory or criticism. It is a reminder that Gregory was, throughout his life, a self-conscious literary artist, who had, in his youth, committed himself to devote his powers of speech to the living Word.[11] In this poem, Gregory answers various accusers who maintain that his writing of

---

[10]The call to self-knowledge was an important theme in ascetical literature, a Christian appropriation of the Delphic Oracle, *Gnothi seauton*—"Know thyself"— which had long served as a summons to the philosophic life. See, for example, Basil, *Homily on the words, "Give heed to thyself"* (*Homilia in illud, Attende tibi ipsi,* translated by Sister M. Monica Wagner, *Saint Basil, Ascetical Works* [New York: Fathers of the Church, 1950], 431–446); and Clement of Alexandria, *Paedagogus,* 3.1: "It seems, then, that the greatest of all lessons is to know oneself. For if one knows oneself, one will know God; and, knowing God, one will be made like God." (In Ante-Nicene Fathers, 2, p. 271). As the call to self-knowledge was only a first step in the Christian life, perhaps this third group of poems, those revolving about the question "Who am I?", correspond to the initial stage of Conversion, while the second and first groups of poems correspond, respectively, to the stages of *praxis* and *theoria,* action and contemplation. Cf. Gregory's Or. 20.12 (PG 35:1080): *Praxis gar epibasis theorias,* the ascent to contemplation is by keeping the commandments.

[11]Cf. poem 2.1.1, *De rebus suis,* lines 96–101: "The fame that goes with letters was the only thing that absorbed me. East and West combined to procure me that, and Athens, the glory of Greece. I labored much for a long time in the craft of letters; but even these two I laid prostrate before the feet of Christ in subjection to the Word of the great God. It overshadows all the twisted, variegated products of the human mind." Cited from D. M. Meehan, trans., *St Gregory of Nazianzus, Three Poems* (Washington, D.C., 1987), 28. Other places where Gregory gives remarks on literary theory are in poem 2.1.12,262–329 (Meehan, ibid., 57–59), and in letters 51–54, to his nephew Nicobulus (found in Nicene and Post-Nicene Fathers, series 2, vol. 7, pp. 476 f.).

verse is undignified and frivolous, that it is done only for the sake
of winning empty fame. He answers these accusations by outlining
four chief reasons for his writing of poetry.

Why Gregory wrote poems

It is worth noting, first of all, the word Gregory uses in this poem to
designate his poetry. The title, *On His Own Verses,* is a traditional
but not very satisfactory rendering of the Greek *Eis ta emmetra.* A
more literal translation might be "On writings in meter." Even that
fails to capture all the implications of the title; the word *metron*
means both "meter" and "measure" (in the sense of moderation). So,
the first reason Gregory gives as to why he writes in meter is that it
helps him to subdue his own "unmeasuredness," i.e., his tendency to
talk too much (vv. 33–37). That the "unmeasuredness" of his tongue
was a real concern to Gregory is indicated by the vow of silence he
took during Lent of 382, when he communicated with others only by
sign-language.[12] This first reason seems to imply that, for Gregory,
the challenge of fitting his thought to meter was an essential part
of what poetry-writing was all about. This brings to mind a remark
once made by Robert Frost, in answer to a question why he didn't
write in free verse: that, while he didn't look down on poets who
chose that medium, it held no attractions for him, for it would be
like "playing tennis without a net."

The word *emmetra* with which Gregory describes his verse
may also indicate something about what he conceived his poetry
to be. The word refers simply to a certain regularity of form, not to
any specific content. It suggests that Gregory may have thought of
his verse as distinguished from his prose, not by some essentially
different content, but by a mere difference in form. In this respect,
his views on poetry are in sharp contrast to those of Aristotle, who
derided didactic verse and saw poetry as necessarily different in

[12] See his poem *On silence at the time of fasting,* poem 2.1.34, translated by
Carolinne White, *Gregory of Nazianzus, Autobiographical Poems* (Cambridge,
1996),,164–81.

content than prose,[13] and are closer to those of Horace, who himself wrote a treatise in verse and considered that poetry best which both instructs and delights.[14]

The second reason Gregory gives for his poetry is that it is meant for young people, to give them spiritual guidance in a form agreeable to them. The notion that poetry is a means of "sweetening . . . the commandments' tartness" (v. 41) is met with also in a sermon by Basil the Great on the first Psalm. The passage is worth quoting:

> For since the Holy Spirit saw the human race sluggish towards virtue and that, from our addiction to pleasure, we took no interest in the right way of life, what did he do? He mixed in the joy of melody with his doctrines, so that by the gentleness and the easiness of the hearing we might take in unconsciously what is helpful from the words: just so, wise doctors, when administering bitter medicines to those who are ill, often spread honey on the rim of the cup. This is the cause for which these harmonious melodies of the Psalms have been made known to us: so that those who are children in years, or rather all who are immature in character, might seem, on the one hand, only to make melody, while in reality having their souls edified.[15]

Gregory, thus, seems to have agreed with Basil that music and poetry can be "a genial vehicle for the good, informing morals by way of melodies" (vv. 86 f.). The question may be raised, however, whether Gregory's views on Christian poetry were in agreement with Basil's in all respects. One scholar, Celica Milovanovic-Barham, has recently suggested that they were not.[16] She thinks that, in vv. 37–46 of this poem, Gregory distinguishes between two classes of his poetry, the first type meant to "sweeten" instruction (v. 41), the second type being in a more "relaxed" mode (v. 42). In Plato's

[13]Cf. Aristotle, *Poetics,* 1447a18–20.

[14]Cf. Horace, *Ars Poetica,* v. 333.

[15]Basil, *Homilia in primum Psalmum,* 1–2, PG 29:212–13.

[16]See her article, "Gregory of Nazianzus: Ars Poetica (*In suos versus:* Carmen 2.1.39)," *Journal of Early Christian Studies,* 5.4 (1997), 497–510, esp. 505 ff.

Republic, Socrates identifies two modes as "relaxed," the Ionian and the Lydian. He notes that they are also called "the soft or drinking harmonies," and deems them unfit for instilling the right discipline into the guardians of his ideal society.[17] Likewise Basil rejected this sort of music as more suitable for drinking-party entertainment than for moral edification.[18] Aristotle, however, seems to have approved of its occasional use.[19] Milovanovic-Barham thinks that, in this instance, Gregory agreed with Aristotle more than with Plato and Basil, and conjectures that, of Gregory's poems, those most likely to have been written in this "relaxed" style are the poems which "most often dwell on the unbearable difficulty of human existence"[20]—that is, those which we have identified as dealing with the question "Who am I?" This is, to say the least, an interesting hypothesis. Milanovic-Barham's interpretation of these poems as serving a function akin to popular music is an appealing one,[21] although more evidence would be needed fully to substantiate the assertion that such a use of poetry represents a real difference in outlook between Gregory and Basil.

The third reason Gregory gives for his writing of poetry is, as he says, "to see to it / that strangers have no advantage over us in literature" (vv. 48 f.). He acknowledges that he is a little embarrassed to admit that such considerations weigh so heavily with him. The lines

[17]Plato, *Republic,* 398e.

[18]Milovanovic-Barham cites a passage from Basil's *Commentary on Isaiah* 5.158, in which Basil condemns the pastime of watching women playing the lyre instead of watching them weaving at the loom ("Gregory Nazianzus: Ars Poetica," 507). It might be noted that not everyone regards the *Commentary on Isaiah* as by Basil, nor is it clear that the passage cited indicates a complete condemnation of lyre music, for it may not be the mode that is condemned, so much as the eyeing of a sultry *chanteuse.* Passages equally condemnatory of voluptuary musical practices could be cited from Gregory's poetry; see, for instance, poem 1.2.8, *A Comparison of Lives,* vv. 99–105.

[19]See his *Politics* 1339b40–1342b34. Aristotle thinks that the relaxed modes "enfeeble the mind" (1340b1); however, he acknowledges that relaxation has its rightful place in life, and that such modes, thus, have a legitimate function (1341 b40). Interestingly, Aristotle seems to think that the relaxed modes have a special appropriateness to old age (1342b27–32).

[20]Milovanovic-Barham, "Gregory Nazianzus: Ars Poetica," 509.

[21]"And what he means by 'songs and musical arrangements' could represent ... some sort of Christian rock, or Christian contemporary music." Ibid., 505f.

suggest that, even in his old age, the threat to Christianity once posed by his old schoolmate, Julian the Apostate, still rankled in Gregory's mind.[22] There were cultural skirmishes in the fourth-century world, quite as much as in contemporary America; questions of language and education, as now, figured heavily in them. Gregory's poems are, on one level at least, documentary evidence of this conflict, a Christian response to a pagan claim that pagans had exclusive proprietary rights to Greek culture. To frame trinitarian doctrine in the form of homeric verse might seem, nowadays, an eccentric and ineffective way of conveying one's message; it was not so, however, in the days when Homer's writings were a cornerstone of the whole educational system, and when some were claiming these writings as pagan religious texts, belonging to the pagans alone. To write trinitarian poems in homeric verse in the late fourth century was to make an implicit claim that the language, with its history and literary forms, was common property, and that Christians could use it as legitimately, and artfully, as anybody else.

Gregory's fourth and final reason for writing verse is that it is to him "a consolation, like an aged swan / to speak to myself with sibilant wings, / not a dirge, but a song of transition."[23] This seems a more private and inward reason than some of the others already mentioned. One wonders whether the four reasons Gregory has enumerated are stated in something like an order of decreasing utilitarian interest, or, perhaps, increasing subjectivity. The first reason, introduced with a pun, seems essentially trivial: Gregory writes verse for his own sake, but the end for which he writes (curbing his tongue) could undoubtedly be effected just as well by other means. The second and third reasons propose, as purposes for which he writes, the salutary or remedial effects of his verse upon other people: in the one case, the salutary effect of teaching the young, in the other, the remedial effect of deflating pagan self-importance (and,

---

[22]Gregory recalls Julian as having said: "To us who worship the gods pertain letters and facility in Greek: to you pertain irrationality and boorishness, and 'Believe!' is all your wisdom." (Or. 4.102).

[23]Vv. 55–57; compare poem 1.2.14,3–4.

perhaps, the positive satisfaction of seeing the pagans outdone). The fourth reason, like the first, is for his own sake, but, unlike the first reason, it is non-trivial: it is important to him at this moment when life is drawing to a close to be honest with himself,and express this inner dialogue openly in verse. Perhaps one should emphasize what he says at the end of the passage; his swan song is "not a dirge, but a song [literally, a hymn] of transition." For all his problems, there is no defeatism in Gregory's life: he knew that, in Christ, he had victory over everything.[24]

Other recent work on Gregory's poetry

As mentioned already, Gregory managed to write a substantial amount of poetry. The 2978 lines here translated represent only a small fraction of some 19,000 lines extant; and these, in turn, may represent only a portion of what he actually wrote; Jerome and Suidas report a total of 30,000 lines.[25] Though not all of what remains is of equal merit, enough of it is worthwhile, whether as literature or for our knowledge of Gregory's life, that it is a shame that more of it isn't translated into modern languages. The effort to translate Gregory's poems into English has made considerable progress over the past fifteen years. The earliest known translation into English of any of his poems was done by an English priest named Thomas Drant, published in 1568 under the title, *Epigrams and sentences spirituall in vers, of GREGORI NAZANZEN, an auncient & famous Bishop in the Greke church.* Drant's translations are in rhyming verse, in rich, expressive Tudor English; what they lack in accuracy and intelligibility is more than made up for by the vividness of the verse.[26]

A few translations of short passages of Gregory's poetry were done in the nineteenth century by Elizabeth Barrett Browning and

[24]See, for example, poem 1.2.15,16of.: "But I, having left off all, retain one thing: the cross of my life, a shining pillar."

[25]Jerome, *On Famous Men,* 117; Suidas, *Lexicon,* tome 1, p.496.

[26]Only two or three copies of Drant's book are extant; it would be a great service to scholarship if it were transcribed and republished.

by Cardinal Newman, among others. Early in the twentieth century a translation of Gregory's epigrams appeared in volume two of the Loeb edition of *The Greek Anthology* (London 1917), done by W. R. Paton. Then came a hiatus until the end of the twentieth century. In the mid-1980s there appeared two works: a booklet containing translations of some of Gregory's poems, including poem 1.1.2, *On the Son*, by John McGuckin,[27] and a prose translation of *Concerning His Own Life* and two other long poems, by Dennis Malaise Meehan, O.S.B.[28] In the 1990s, two more major translations appeared: a free-verse translation of the poem *Concerning His Own Life* and of four other autobiographical poems, by Carolinne White, published in the Cambridge Medieval Classics series[29]; and a prose translation, with commentary, of the *Poemata Arcana* by D. A. Sykes, together with a critical edition of the Greek text by Claudio Moreschini, in the Oxford Theological Monograph series.[30]

Most of the translations in this volume were originally done as part of a dissertation submitted to the Catholic University of America in 1994,[31] and have not substantially been changed since then.

[27]John A. McGuckin, trans., *Saint Gregory Nazianzen: Selected Poems* (Fairacres, Oxford: Sisters of the Love of God Press, 1986).

[28]Dennis Molaise Meehan, trans., *Saint Gregory of Nazianzus. Three Poems: Concerning His Own Affairs, Concerning Himself and the Bishops, Concerning His Own Life,* Fathers of the Church, 75 (Washington, D.C.: Catholic University of America Press, 1987). According to Rosemary Radford Ruether, who used this translation of Meehan's in manuscript form when writing her own study of Gregory in the 1960s, Meehan also did a translation of Gregory's letters 1–101, while, under his supervision, she completed the work with a translation of letters 102–244 (see her *Gregory of Nazianzus, Rhetor and Philosopher* [Oxford, 1969], 17); none of this, sadly, has ever been published.

[29]Carolinne White, ed. and trans., *Gregory of Nazianzus, Autobiographical Poems,* Cambridge Medieval Classics, 6 (Cambridge: Cambridge University Press, 1996).

[30]Claudio Moreschini ed. and D. A. Sykes trans., *St Gregory of Nazianzus: Poemata Arcana* (Oxford: Clarendon Press, 1997).

[31]P. Gilbert, *Person and Nature in the Theological Poems of St Gregory of Nazianzus* (Ph.D. Diss., Catholic University of America, Washington D.C., 1995). The exceptions are the poems *In Praise of Virginity* (poem 1.2.1), *Concerning the Genuine Books of Divine Scripture* (poem 1.1.12), *On Different Walks of Life* (poem 1.2.16), and *Blessings of Various Lives* (poem 1.2.17).

The translations were all made from the old, non-critical (though generally reliable) texts in Migne, with the exception of 60 extra lines assigned to poem 1.1.9, edited by Bernhard Wyss.[32] One of the chief justifications of this volume is that it is intended to fulfil some of the purposes for which Gregory originally wrote his verse. He meant his poems to be read by young people, i.e., non-specialists, beginners, as a guide to Christian life and thought. The only qualifications he sets for those who are to read his poems are that they be "pure, or being purified" (poem 1.1.1, 10; cf. poem 1.2.1, 7–10). He writes, in other words, for the faithful, maybe even for those who would dearly like to be faithful, whatever their level of progress in understanding. I have tried, in translating these poems, to catch something of Gregory's spirit, and to put them into something like a form into which Gregory might have put them had he spoken American English at the end of the twentieth century. Such a procedure might be condemned as subjective and lacking in scientific methodology, yet, as this is an attempt to translate poems, and poems of a saint, some such method seemed to be called for.

A word about theology

So far, very little has been said in this Introduction about Gregory's theology, which may seem odd in view of the fact that we are considering the poems of one who is called "the Theologian." A long statement would be out of place here, but it is worth noting briefly the relationship between Gregory's personal experience and his theology, to gain the right perspective upon his poems.

The truer artistic impulses in Gregory's poetry seem to arise out of a need for communion, which can only be fully satisfied by communion with the triune God. The personal character of Gregory's poetry is not accidental, nor simply rhetorical; it flows from the nature of Christian experience. Within Christianity, God, who is

[32]Bernhard Wyss, "Zu Gregor von Nazianz," in *Phyllobolia, für P. von der Mühil* (Basel, 1946), 153–83.

tri-personal, can be experienced only in a personal way—can be known only by communion with the living God in Jesus Christ. Gregory's theology, his debates with Arians and Neo-Arians, with Pneumatomachians and Apollinarians, is all about that communion, and his poetry—perhaps especially those poems in which the question of his own being is paramount—flows from it. But the nature of Christian experience raises important questions about God himself. What must God be, if our experience of him is personal? Who must Jesus Christ be, if he is able to effect communion between us and the living God, if he is able to restore that communion after it has been broken? Who, or what, is the Holy Spirit? Or again, what must the world be, if it holds together over time—what relationship to God does that imply? Is it explainable on its own terms, or does it, in its contingency, point to someone else as its necessary source? By what means does God govern the creation? Do things just happen randomly, or for a purpose? If all things are the creation of a good God, why are some things evil? What are angels? What role do they serve in God's creation? What is the human soul? For what purpose did God create a being who is partly material, partly spiritual? And when such a being had fallen away from God, what did God do to restore him to that state which he had lost? These are the questions we find Gregory asking in his theological poems, and the same questions are implied in his more personal, autobiographical poems, those poems in which he asks the question "Who am I?" He cannot, in fact, answer the question "Who am I?" unless he takes all these other questions into account.

But it would be impossible, in a brief introduction like this, to go through all the answers Gregory supplies to these various questions: it would require a long volume, perhaps many long volumes, perhaps a whole library. Fortunately, that effort is unnecessary. If, to understand any text, a commentary were always needed, then we would face what Aristotle calls an infinite regression: we would always be in need of another book to explain the one before, and there would be no starting place. Gregory seems to have meant his poems as a starting place. He wrote them for beginners. Although requiring thought, they are not unintelligible. For this reason, the reader is advised to seek the meaning of Gregory's theology in the poems themselves, in the expectation that their value also as poetry will be found in one's so doing.

Brief chronology of St Gregory's life

325 Gregory's father, the elder Gregory, is converted to Christianity through the influence of his wife, Nonna. Not long afterward, he is ordained bishop of the city of Nazianzus, in Cappadocia.

329/30 Gregory the Theologian born, probably at Arianzus near Nazianzus, the second of three children (an older sister Gorgonia and a younger brother Caesarius).

c.345 Gregory, attending boarding school at Caesarea in Cappadocia, meets Basil for the first time.

c.348 Gregory, accompanied at first by his brother, begins his travels abroad to acquire a higher education. First goes to Caesarea in Palestine, attends the catechetical school there founded by Origen in the third century. Then travels to Alexandria; Caesarius stays there, but Gregory departs for Athens.

c.349 During a sea-voyage to Athens, Gregory's ship is nearly lost in a storm. He renews his commitment to God.

c.349–58 Studies at Athens; becomes close friends with Basil; meets Julian, the future emperor and apostate. Perfects his oratorical techniques.

c.359 On returning to Nazianzus, is baptized by his father. Undergoes the first of many crises. Decides to pursue a "middle way" of life, an ascetical life in the midst of the world. Occasional visits to Basil's monastery in Pontus, where Basil and Gregory collaborate on the *Philocalia,* a compilation of extracts from the writings of Origen and on Basil's monastic *Rules.*

360–3 Julian as emperor attempts to restore paganism as the official Roman religion; proscribes Christians from serving as teachers.

362 Gregory is ordained, against his will, by his father. Runs away to Basil's monastery; returns after three months, delivers Easter sermon and his *Apology for His Flight to Pontus,* a kind of treatise on the Christian priesthood.

364 Basil ordained priest in Caesarea.

368 Death of Caesarius and Gorgonia.

370 Basil elected archbishop of Caesarea. Division by the Emperor Valens of Cappadocia into two civil dioceses causes a schism between Basil and Anthimus of Tyana, who claims metropolitan rights for his see.

372 Basil and the elder Gregory consecrate Gregory, against his will, as bishop of Sasima, a strategically important town with no redeeming qualities on the borderland between Basil's and Anthimus' territories. Gregory attempts to occupy his see and is physically assaulted by Anthimus' men. Gregory withdraws to the mountain; is finally persuaded by his father to serve at Nazianzus as adjutant bishop. The affair produces a chill in Gregory's and Basil's friendship.

374 Death of Gregory's parents, Gregory the elder and Nonna. Gregory, unable to persuade the clergy of the region to elect a new bishop for Nazianzus, retires to Seleucia, where he serves as spiritual director to a women's monastery (Convent of St Thekla). Probably writes some of his ethical poetry at this time, e.g., the poem *In Praise of Virginity.*

378 Death of the Arian emperor Valens changes the religious situation. At a Council in Antioch, a missionary outreach to Constantinople is planned. Gregory is called upon to head it.

379 Death of Basil, January 1. Sometime before Easter, Gregory arrives at Constantinople. Resides at the house of his cousin, Theodosia,

one room of which is set apart for an Orthodox chapel, which is given the name "Anastasia" ("Resurrection"). Gregory's preaching soon draws large crowds, and many enemies.

380 Maximus the Cynic, after winning Gregory's confidence, betrays him and attempts to take over the Church of Constantinople; secretly consecrated at night by some Egyptian bishops; the people drive him out of town; he eventually goes West to seek ecclesiastical support.

mid-380 Gregory delivers the *Five Theological Orations.*

380 November 24: Emperor Theodosius, a Nicene Christian, enters Constantinople, evicts the Arians from the churches, has Gregory installed at the cathedral as bishop.

381 May–June. The Second Ecumenical Council. Chaired at first by Meletius of Antioch. After Gregory's position as Archbishop of Constantinople is confirmed, Meletius dies; Gregory is elected to succeed him as president of the Council. Gregory proposes to end the Schism of Antioch by recognizing Paulinus, Meletius' rival, as bishop; the proposal is angrily rejected. Gregory probably sits out, due to illness, the sessions of the Council that dealt with the question of the Holy Spirit. When Western and Egyptian delegations arrive at the Council, they object to Gregory's serving as archbishop of Constantinople, citing Canon 15 of Nicaea and the fact that Gregory had previously been consecrated as bishop of Sasima. Rather than argue the point, Gregory resigns. Delivers a *Farewell Oration,* then returns to Cappadocia. Retires to his family home at Arianzus, to recuperate physically and emotionally.

late 381 Gregory writes some of his major autobiographical poems, e.g., the *De Vita Sua,* to give his own account of the events that led to his withdrawal from Constantinople. Much of the *Poemata Arcana* probably written about this time.

382 January 1. Gregory delivers a memorial oration *On the Great Basil* at Caesarea, on the third anniversary of his friend's death.

382 Lent. Gregory observes a vow of silence during the 40 days of the fast.

Summer. Gregory briefly undertakes to govern the Church of Nazianzus till a successor to his father can be found. Addresses the problem of Apollinarian propaganda in a series of christological letters, e.g., the *First* and *Second Letters to Cledonius* (epist. 101 and 102). The poem *On the Incarnation, Against Apollinarius* (poem 1.1.10) probably also written at this time.

383 Gregory's health worsens; he visits hot baths at Xanxaris. In his absence, Apollinarians elect their own bishop of Nazianzus. Gregory calls on the secular arm to evict them.

mid-year: A minor civil insurrection in Nazianzus has Gregory interceding for the city to the authorities (epist. 141).

end of the year: Gregory's cousin Eulalius is elected new bishop of Nazianzus. Gregory is allowed to go into full retirement.

384–389/90 Gregory lives a secluded monastic life at his home at Arianzus. Edits his orations; produces editions of his own and Basil's letters; writes reams of verse. Probably the poems *On Human Nature* and *On the Cheapness of the Outward Man* are written during this time, along with much of the rest of the personal poetry. Events in Gregory's life during these years are hard to reconstruct. He writes many letters to friends and relatives. Is generally held in high regard. At some point, noisy, offensive neighbors cause him to leave home (epist. 203); whether he returns is uncertain.

392 Jerome, writing his *On Famous Men,* reports that Gregory has been dead for three years. Thus, his death is generally assigned to 389/390. His remains, interred at Arianzus, are later taken to Constantinople; at some point in the Middle Ages his body is taken to Rome, where it rests in a chapel unto itself.

Outlines of Major Poems

The
Poems

On the Father

Poem 1.1.1, De Patre (PG 37:397–401)

I know we are as though making a great voyage on a raft,
or hastening towards the starry sky upon small wings,
when, with such poems, mind has moved to exhibit the
    Godhead   (398)
(which transcends the power of heavenly beings to worship as
    is due),
5 or the great Godhead's statutes, and the universe's helm.
Nevertheless, since God is often not as pleased by the
    gift   (399)
of the worse majority, as by that of the beloved few,
for this reason I take courage to break forth into speech. But
    flee
from afar, whoever is a sinner; my speech is directed
10 either to the pure, or to them that are being purified. But
infidels, like wild beasts, when on the high-peaked mountain
Christ shone forth and wrote the law for Moses upon tables,
were immediately overcome beneath the broken crags.
So much for the likes of these; thus also the Word expelled
15 the worst ones of our company, who had a heart opposed to
    God.
But as for me, I will set down this preface on sundry leaves, a
    voice
instilling an uncouth people with fear, uttered of old
by witnesses of words, men of godly minds,

    Moses and Isaiah (I'll speak to those who have
        knowledge),   (400)
20 who gave the law, the one new-formed, the other when it was
        broken.
    "Let the heavens give ear, and let the earth receive my words."
    O Spirit of God, may you then waken my mind and tongue
    as a loud-shouting clarion of truth, so that all
    may rejoice, who are united in spirit to the entire Godhead.
25 There is one God, without beginning or cause, not limited
    by anything existing before, or afterward to be,
    encompassing the aeons, and infinite; the noble,
    great, only-begotten Son's great Father; who had, in the
    Son, no suffering of anything fleshly, since he is mind. One
        other
30 is God, not other in Godhead, God's Word, who is
    his living paternal seal, the sole
    Son of him who has no origin, and most Unique from the
        Unique, equal   (401)
    in might, so that, while the one remains the whole parent, the
        Son
    is world-maker, lawgiver, the Father's strength and intellect.
35 There is one Spirit, God from God who is good. Be gone all of
        you
    whom the Spirit has not sealed so as to show forth his
        Godhead,
    but are either rotten to the core, or have a vile tongue:
    half-shining, invidious, clever self-taught people,
    a covered-up fountain, a lamp in a murky crevice.

On the Son

Poem 1.1.2, De Filio (PG 37:401–408)

First of all we shall sing the Son, honoring that blood
that is our passions' cleansing. For we must come to the
mortal's aid with those of heaven, due to   (402)
that tongue that wars against the divine: foul-minded, suicidal.
5   Before the great Father, nothing was. For he holds within
        himself
everything, and nothing higher than the Father exists. He who
        has sprung
from the Father is the great God's Word: eternal Son,
the archetype's image, a nature equal to his parent.
For the Son so great is the Father's glory, and from him he
        shone forth,
10   as only the Father and he that shone forth from the Father
        understand.
For no one has come close to the Godhead; but this much at
        least
is clear to everyone, just as it is to me:
I have no right to foist on the Godhead a birthday,
an emission, or some loathsome cutting. For though I do not
        reproduce
15   dispassionately, since I'm composite, not at all subject to
        passion   (403)
is he who is wholly incomposite, unbodied. When things'
natures are remote, what wonder if their beginnings differ, too?
If time came before me, time is not before

39

the Word, whose begetter is atemporal. When the
        beginningless
20 Father was there, leaving nothing superior to his divinity,
    then also was there the Father's Son, having in the Father a
            timeless beginning,
    like the sun's great circle of overwhelming clear light.
    And, while all ideas fall short of the great God,
    so that nothing interposes between Father and Son,
25 eternally existing, we should distinguish the Lord the
    Son from the Lord the Father. If something came prior to God,
    whether time, or will, that would divide the Godhead, I think.
    To be God, to be begetter, he must be the great begetter.
        And if the greatest   (404)
    thing concerning the Father is that his treasured divinity has
        no origin,
30 it's no less a thing for the honored offspring of the great Father
    to have such a root. So don't exclude God from God.
    For you've not known the Child distanced from the Father. The
        terms
    "unbegotten" and "begotten of the Father" do not make
    two kinds of Godhead. Someone has alleged about this that
35 each is foreign to the other, but the nature is inseparable, if you
        ask me.
    Then, though the Word is begotten, he is not fleshly,
    since his Father, it will be admitted, is fleshless (and no man's
        mind
    is ever so corrupt as to think otherwise).
    And so you have God the Son, his parent's worthy pride and
        joy.
40 But if, rendering offerings to the great Father's Godhead
    worthlessly, and gravening in your heart a hollow fear,
    you'd deny this thing, and would hurl Christ out amongst
        creatures,   (405)
    you insult, O nitwit, the divinity of them both:

you filch the Son's, who's not God if created.
45 For all that once was not is but a creature, even if a thing
    perdures, and stands as fixed, through God's great reasons.
    And why, bold sir, when your starting point was this,
    that, through Christ's sufferings, you may become god
         hereafter,
    do you then make him go in chains, and call him your co-slave,
50 honoring him with gifts for slavery, instead of for being God?
    If the great God formed him later, as a fine tool
    (as a smith forges a hammer for the sake of a cart),
    so that, by his Firstborn's hand, God might make me,
    then far worthier than the celestial Christ would be
55 the creature, if for its sake the Word exists,   (406)
    not it for Christ. Who would maintain such a thing?
    But if it's that, to rescue you from your passions, he took on a
         body,
    would you therefore set a yardstick on his great-famed
         Godhead?
    Has he sinned, in pitying you? To me, rather, he's the more
         amazing.
60 For he didn't shave off any bit of Godhead, and still he saved
         me,
    stooping as a doctor over my foul-smelling passions.
    He was a man, but God. David's offspring, but Adam's
    Maker. A bearer of flesh, but, even so, beyond all body.
    From a mother, but she a virgin. Comprehensible, but
         immeasurable.
65 And a manger received him, while a star led
    the Magi, who so came bearing gifts, and fell on bended knee.
    As a man he entered the arena, but he prevailed, as
         indomitable,
    over the tempter in three bouts. Food was set before him, (407)
    but he fed thousands, and changed the water into wine.

70   He got baptized, but he washed sins clean, but he was
            proclaimed
     by the Spirit, in a voice of thunder, to be the Son of the One
            Uncaused.
     As a man he took rest, and as God he put to rest the sea.
     His knees were wearied, but he bolstered the strength and
            knees of the lame.
     He prayed, but who was it who heard the petitions of the
            feeble?
75   He was the sacrifice, but the high priest: making an offering,
            but himself God.
     He dedicated his blood to God, and cleansed the entire world.
     a cross carried him up, while the bolts nailed fast sin.
     But what's it for me to say these things? He had company with
            the dead,
     but he rose from the dead, and the dead, the bygone, he raised
            up:
80   there a mortal's poverty, here the incorporeal' s wealth.
     Don't you dishonor, then, his divinity on account of his
            human things,   (408)
     but, for the divine's sake, hold in renown the earthly form
     into which, thoughtful towards you, he formed himself, the
            incorruptible Son.

On the Holy Spirit

Poem 1.1.3, De Spiritu Sancto (PG 37:408–415)

Soul, why delay? Sing also the Spirit's glory,
and don't separate in speech what the nature did not leave out.
Let us quake before the great Spirit, who is my God, who's
    made me know God,
who is God there above, and who forms God here:
5 almighty, imparting manifold gifts, him whom the holy choir
    hymns,
who brings life to those in heaven and on earth, and is
    enthroned on high,
coming from the Father, the divine force, self-commandeered;
he is not a Child (for there is one worthy Child of the One
    who's best),
nor is he outside the unseen Godhead, but of identical
    honor.   (409)
10 Now, if someone seeks to understand the heavenly Spirit's
    divinity
through the pages of divinely-inspired Law,
he shall see many ways, close-packed, collected into one,
if he has yearned, and gathered something of the
Holy Ghost with his heart, and if his piercing mind has
    perceived.
1 But if he seeks a plain assertion of his beloved divinity,
let him known this, he seeks unsensibly. For it wouldn't have
    been right,

when Christ's own hadn't yet appeared to most of
    humankind,
to lay on feeble hearts a weight of doubt.
For, with beginners, it's not the time
20 for more consummate language. Who shows a fire's
    whole glow
to still-dim eyes, or gorges them with light insatiable?
It's better if, bit by bit, you bring on the fiery glowings,
lest you even hurt some way the springs of a sweeter
    light.   (410)
For, as of old the Scriptures displayed the whole deity
25 of the royal Father, and Christ's great fame began to dawn,
disclosed to men of little understanding,
so also, later when the Son's shone more distinctly,
the brightness of the Spirit's deity glowed.
Now to them he gave a small illumination, while most he left
    to us,
30 even distributing himself to us later in tongues of fire
betokening divinity, after the Savior had gone up from the
    earth.
For I, too, have known God to be as fire to the wicked, and as
    light to the good.
There, I have gathered up the Godhead for you. But if you're
    left speechless,
hearing how a Son and one who's not Son share one Godhead,
35 as though being swayed two ways, by two good arguments,
God himself, I trust, shall come forth next to give a reason.
From the one first father sprang a wife and Seth,   (411)
she a half-slice, he a second child by marriage bonds,
one not by birth, the other by birth, but both being equally
    human.
40 Remembering these, don't you belittle any within the
    Godhead,

putting this one above, this one below. One is the nature,
  immeasurable,
uncreated, a-temporal, excellent, free, and co-venerable,
one God in three refulgences, making the world go round.
By these I am awakened, another new young man, when in the
  font
45 death gets buried, and I come back racing to the light.
For the threefold Godhead made me rise out a light-bearer.
No, beloved cleansing, I won't falsify you. If, having been
  washed
in the divinity, I should divide the bright divinity,   (412)
it would have been better if . . . but I shudder to complete an
  evil sentence,
50 by my hope in the divine gift, and in the baths.
If he has fully cleansed the whole of me, the whole God then is
venerable, so I feel. But whatever man's a sinner can assert the
  inequality,
cutting himself asunder from God's gift, his own divinity.
And if we hear some things about either the Child or the good
55 Spirit, in divine words and from God-bearing
men, as, that they hold a second place to God the Father,
I charge you so to understand this, by words of wisdom's
  untold depths:
that it refers to the unoriginate root, it doesn't split
the Godhead, so that you've got one sole power, not
  worshipped severally.
60 From unity is the Trinity, and from Trinity again the: (413)
  unity
not as a source, a spring, a mighty river, sharing a single
  current,
in three separate manners traverse the earth;
nor as a torch, taken from a pyre, converges again in one;
nor like a word, both going out from the mind and remaining
  in it;

65 nor like some shimmering of dancing sunbeams off the waters,
a restless gleaming, wavering on the walls,
approaching, then fleeing, fleeing, then drawing near.
For God's nature is not restless, nor flowing,
nor again a coalescing; but what is God's is steadfast.
70 But you might make a pure offering privately, thinking thus.
In threefold lights the one nature is established,
not a numberless unity, since it subsists in three   (414)
    excellencies,
nor a Threesome worshipped severally, since the nature is
    inseparable.
In the Godhead is the unity, but they whose Godhead it is are
    three in number.
75 Each is the one God, if you should talk of them singly.
Again, there is one God, without beginning, whence comes the
    wealth of Godhead
whenever the word refers to all three, so that, on the
one hand, it might reverently proclaim to men the threefold
    lights, and
on the other hand, that by it we might extol the strong-shining
    Monarchy,
80 and not content ourselves with a pluralist marketplace of gods.
For, by me, polyarchy and an utter brawling anarchy are
one and the same. Division is strife, and hastens to
dissolution. For this reason, polyarchy is far from the Godhead, as I take it.
Someone might call them "three gods" if he had divided them
85 by times, intellect, power, or will,   (415)
where none, without brawling, would be identical even with
itself.
But one is the might of my Trinity, one the knowledge,
one the glory, one the power. So, again, the unity cannot
    dissolve,
being greatly honored in the one harmony of divinity.

90 So much radiance has the Trinity revealed to my eyes,
      from the wings and the veil within the divine temple,
      beneath which God's royal nature lies hid. And if something
            extra is
      for the angelic choirs, let the Trinity know what this extra is.

Concerning the World

Poem 1.1.4, De mundo (PG 37:415–423)

Come along, then, let us hymn the great God's creation,
contending against false views.
One is God: but, by contrast, the Greek sages' fable   (416)
is feeble, which makes out matter and the ideas to be, like him,
    without beginning.
5 Now, however many are the sacred forms, which they make to
    be gods,

they were not, but came to be, as the great God willed it.
But whoever saw matter that has no looks, or who has seen an
    immaterial
form, even if he's striven much with a turmoil of mind?
10 For I personally have not seen a colorless body, nor some
    disembodied
color. Who distinguished these things that nature, in com-
    bining them, did not?
Still, let us make the division: consider with me how, if all
    things were once
unblended, they have come together in one, or what world
stood so utterly split apart? But if things were commingled,
how did they get to be mingled? Who mingled them if not
    God? But if God's
15 the mixer, accept him likewise as creator of all.
A potter, too, puts form to his clay when he turns the   (417)
    wheel,
a goldsmith gives it to gold, and a sculptor to stones.

Credit God with more than you do our mind, O lover of no
origins.

Matter is what's more, with the forms that move.

20 He thought, and things came to be, in-formed: the divine
thought

is the complicated womb of all that is. For it's not likely

that, like some painter, he conjured up an image from a similar
image,

having seen beforehand things that his own one mind did not
write.

And as for you, evil darkness of the Manichees, you were not
originally

25 enthroned in opposition to the most high light. If God was,

darkness was not. For it's unthinkable that evil should measure
up with God.

If darkness was, you don't know God. An alliance would be
unseemly;

if they fight, the superior prevails. But if they're equally
strong,

what third one has the know-how to join them and end
their quarrel?   (418)

30 And this is the strangest thing, since you raise up a grim
battle:

you set them back in agreement, you've forgotten the
competition.

I am a soul and body: the one, an efflux of divinity,

of infinite light; the other was formed for you

from a murky root. But these which were far apart, you've
gathered in one.

35 If I am a common nature, I end the battle. If the battle is grim,

continual, then I am no longer a nature woven of them both.

For a child is not from those who battle, but from those who
love.

Such is your obfuscated heart. But for me at least

there is one God, without beginning, not struggling, one
    worthy light,
40   the strength of minds that run aloft, the simple, the
    composite,
the heavenly, the earthly; but darkness came last of all,   (419)
no self-subsistent, circumscribed nature, but our own
evil, this. And evil, too, is the commandment's transgression,
as night is the sun's setting, and old age the debility
45   of youth. And the course of the sun has brought up
fearful winter's cold. The one who was first among heavenly
    lights
destroyed by his presumption light and honor,
and bears eternal enmity to the race of men. And because of
    this murderer
the first mortal also tasted of evil
50   and of death, when he fanned the flames for me by his deceits.
This then is the late-born evil's nature, and such a one
is its father. Now, the decay is a rusting of mighty iron:
but I myself, self-slain, sowed the evil decay   (420)
by following the malignant one's stratagems, by his counsel.
55   If you, world, have been here as long as the Trinity, your fame
should be near to him who has no beginning: why then
do Christ-bearing men, adept in things divine, set you so far
    off,
such that they reckon not a great many years to have rolled by
since the great Word of God created you? Then if you were
    created
60   subsequently, let us consider why the divine thought moved
(for God's not idle, neither imperfect, in my view)
before setting this whole world up, and fashioning it with
    kinds.
When the Most High reigned in empty aeons
he was moved in beholding his beauty's cherished splendor,
65   the like, equivalent radiance of thrice-shining Godhead   (421)

which only to that Godhead, and God's own, is plain to see.
He was moved, too, in observing the world's patterns he'd set
    up,
the world-engendering mind finding in these great thoughts
what was yet to be, which to God, again, was present.
70 All things are immediate to God, as much things future as
    things past,
as well as things now present. Time for me is fractured in this
    way,
with some things earlier, others later: but for God it all comes
    in one,
and the great Godhead engulfs it in his arms.
Therefore give heed to what my mind has hewn.
75 Mind travailed to bring all things to birth, and at last the birth
    broke through,
seasonably, when God's great Word brought it to view.
He wanted, first, to establish the nature of mind, both   (422)
    celestial
and earthly, as a transparent mirror of the primal light:
both gleaming upwards, as the Lord's attendant,
80 full-shining, immense, and directing his fame this way,
fountaining divinity, so that he might both rule over others in
heaven, and be for yet more a light, shedding blessings.
For it's my Lord's own very nature to grant bliss.
But lest creation should encroach on God, yearning for a
    godlike
85 honor, and obliterate light and honor
(since preserving measure is best, but unmeasuredness is
    worst),
therefore, in loving concern for those yet to be, the lofty Word
cast away from the Trinity whatever light lay round the throne,
and human nature away from angelic choirs: the angels'
    nature
90 not too far removed, a helper, but ours   (423)

indeed quite far removed, since our existence is from earth
mixed with divinity, whereas the simpler nature's better.
Now, of these worlds, the firstborn was that other heaven,
the region of those who bear the divine, perceptible to minds
  only,
95 all-luminous; to it the man of God wends his way from here
later, once he's perfected as god, purified in mind and flesh.
But this world is mortal, made for mortals, when it was meant
  to be
set up as a gift of lights, to be a proclamation of God
by its beauty and size, and his image's enthronement;
100 but both the first world and the last are in the great God's
  reckonings.

On Providence

Poem 1.1.5, De Providentia (PG 37:424–429)

On such vast foundations, the endless world was fixed   (424)
    fast
by the great Mind who bears within all things, while over all
he exists; but by what means is this incomprehensibility
    held?
But since its creation, he propels it from its first impulse,
5   like a whirligig driven by a whirlwind's blow,
moving it by mighty, immovable reasons.
For it's not by chance, the nature of such and so great
a world, wherewith nothing comparable can be thought—
do not credit so much to chancy reasons.
10   Who ever saw a house not built by hands?
Who's seen a self-built ship, or a fleet chariot? A shield
    and a helmet?   (425)
Nor would so much have lasted through time, minus a ruler;
and the choir would have stopped, I'd say, without its
    conductor.
Neither is there likely to be another who directs the universe
15   than him who wrought it. But if you add on the stars as
    guides
for our race and our lives and the universe besides,
then tell me, for these stars, do you make another heaven go
    round?
And for this, is there yet another, forever guiding the guides?
One king is co-starred with many others: a good man,

20   a bad one, a rhetor, a merchant, a hobo,
       but the eminent throne can bear this insolence. And at sea
       and in war there comes one common fate to many, who were
           of different births.
       The stars that had bound them did not bind them a common
           end,
       while those they had set apart, the same death joins.   (426)
25   If then each star effects some primary necessity,
       it's a myth; but if, again, this is exerted by some mightier
           conjunction,
       then signs are aligned with signs. So who mixed them?
       For he that combined them could also have dissolved them, if
           he'd wanted.
       But if he's God, how is that first, which God threshed out for
           me?
30   Unless you would even rotate God himself beneath
           your stars!
       But if no one's in control, how will it stand? I don't see how.
       Now these people by such notions keep out God.
       For it's either God who guides, or it's the stars.
       But as for me, I know this much: God governs all these
           things,
35   the Word of God directing, this way and that, everything,
           above or
       below, that he's set up by his thoughts: above, he gave
       harmony and motion and ever-enduring constancy;   (427)
       here, life, changeable and bearing many forms;
       some of which things he's shown to us, others, again, he stores
           in the layaways
40   of his wisdom, in his will to thwart man's hollow boast.
       And some things he's placed right here, others in the
           final days
       shall meet us. A farmer clips off all his fruits in season:
       in the same way, Christ is my life's most expert judge.

This is my doctrine, not astral, self-motivated.
45   But you, tell me of the hours' ascendants and the degrees
     of minutes, of zodiacal circles and the measures of their
         course;
     explain for me, too, the laws of life, and the dread that comes to
         sinners,
     the hope, again, that finally meets the good.
     For if the circle conveys all things, then by its revolution   (428)
50   I'm whisked, and the circle's even caused my very desire:
     neither is there in me some inclination towards what's
         better,
     whether of will or mind, but the firmament has flung me
         such a way.
     Let that angel-star, Christ's mighty fame, keep silent,
     that guided the Magi from the East into the city
55   when Christ shone forth, the eternal Son, a mortal's child.
     For it was not one of those in which the astrologers
     were versed, but a stranger, which had not till then
         appeared,
     but had been foreseen in the Hebraic books, whereby the
         Chaldaean
     children (as many as dealt in stars) had learned of it;
60   so that, when they saw it, among the many they observed,
         alone
     newly radiant, trekking from the East upon the air   (429)
     to the Hebrews' land, they construed it to mean the
         King.
     Then it was that their craft's techniques together fell,
     when, with the stars, the astrologers bowed in worship of the
         King.
65   But these same heavens continue on that way that Christ the
         Lord
     ordained for them: fiery, always running, undeflected,

the fixed stars and the planets, and those whose way
    returns, as it is said:
whether they be of a nature of unconsuming fire, or a body,
a quintessence, as they call it, having a circular course.

70   But we ascend by our own road. For we strive for
a rational and a heavenly nature, even though shackled by the
    earth.

Concerning Spiritual Beings

Poem 1.1.7, De substantiis mente praeditis (PG 37:438–446)

Now as, amidst a clearing, rain-laden air,
meeting the clouds with circulating reflection,   (439)
the sun's ray unwinds a many-colored rainbow,
while, from above, all the ethereal element gleams
5   with manifold circles, which break up further out:
such also is the nature of the lights that radiate always
from the highest light, illuminating lesser intellects with their
    beams.
And truly he is the fountain of lights, the Light that cannot be
    named,
neither grasped, who flees from an intellect swiftly drawing
    near,
10 forever outpacing the wits of all, so that, yearning,
we might struggle anew for what is higher. But these,
      again, are
secondary lights, possessing from the Trinity a royal dignity,
the dazzling angels, invisible, who go therefore about
the great throne, since they are nimble intelligences,
15 fire and divine spirits coursing swiftly through the air,   (440)
hurriedly attending to his great behests:
simple, noetic, translucent, neither coming from
bodies (for bodies, since they are compounds, are again
    destroyed),
nor entering upon bodies, but just what they were originally,
    they remain.

20   I had wanted to say, "altogether unyielding." But hold
          back that horse
      that breathes so hotly, administering the mind's bridle.
      So then, some of these are the great God's attendants;
      others, again, hold sway in all the world, by their
          preservations,
      each one holding from the Lord his own proper dominion,
25   observing men, and cities, and every nation,
      and discerning the reasonable offerings made by mortals.
      Soul of mine, what are you doing? Reason trembles, entering
          upon
      heavenly beauties. But a mist has met up with me,   (441)
      and I can no better carry this discourse forward than
          retract it.
30   And as when some wayfarer, coming to a violent stream,
      suddenly jumps back, and is stopped despite his longing,
      with his mind in much uneasiness regarding the current:
      need strengthens courage, but fear inhibits desire;
      often he'll raise on the water the sole of his foot, and often
          again
35   he shrinks back, till, in their struggle, necessity triumphs over
          fear—
      so likewise, when I draw close to the unseen deity,
      I dread to propose that those who attend the pure One who
          rules on high,
      a species filled with light, might sin,
      lest I should so smooth out for many a path of evil.
40   But I dread inscribing by my words a changeless good
      when I see, all the while, a twisted one ruling over evil.   (442)
      For it was not from the one who's good, to plant in us
          an evil nature,
      or to bring forth strife and hatreds to his friends;
      nor did he erect a rivaling throne of villainy
45   later, or one having an unoriginate nature like the Lord's.

So, in my anguish, God put this kind of mind in me.
So first of all, the Godhead's hallowed nature always was
     unchanging,
never a many instead of one. For what is better than divinity,
that he should shift to it? Something extra were a flight from
     what he is.
50 Second are the great assistants of the highest light,
as close to the prototype's splendor as is
ether to the sun. The third-place atmosphere is us.
Changeless is God's nature in all things, the angels' is   (443)
hard to turn towards evil, while ours, coming third, changes
     easily,
55 being as far remote from God as from what's wicked.
For this cause Lucifer, chief in rank, being loftily lifted up
(for, so it was, he hoped for the great God's royal honor,
though he had high fame), obliterated his splendor,
and plummeted dishonored thither, nor a God, but utter
     darkness.
60 And, from the cloddy ground on which, though weightless, he
     had fallen,
he utterly hates the wise of heart, and shuts off
all heaven's ways, maddened at his disfigurement.
Nor did he wish God's creature to draw near to the divinity
whence he'd fallen, since he longed to have humans with him
     in a
65 common sin and darkness. Because of this he cast them out of
     paradise,
the envier, in his lust for a glory equaling God's.   (444)
This, then, was how the one aloft fell out from heaven's vault.
But he didn't slip alone, but after arrogance destroyed him
there fell with him a multitude, as many as he'd schooled in evil
70 (as when some criminal breaks away an army from its king),
both through envy of the godly-minded choir that rules above
and because of the desire of most of these fiends for power.

Therefore there sprang from them evil beings on earth,
demons, minions to the murderous king of evil:
75   languors, shades, ill-boding phantasms of the night,
liars and revilers, instructors in sin,
bamboozlers, souses, seducers, party-animals,
soothsayers, riddlers, warmongers, the bloody,
the hellish, the lurking, the shameless, the high impostors,
80   who beckon on approaching, but hate when hauling off: (445)
as night or as a light, so that they may capture, blatantly
    or by stealth.
Such is the army of these, and such, again, is their
    commander;
but simply to do away with him was not what Christ had in
    mind,
in that will of his by which he made the entire world—and to
    annihilate him
85   he had only to wish on a sudden (it is hard to elude the wrath
    of God);
neither, though, did he let my enemy go scot-free,
but he set him loose halfway, between the good and the evil,
and gave him bitter strife on either side, so as to have a
    dreadful
shame also in this, that he must fight his own subordinates,
90   and so that strugglers for virtue should have eternal glory,
like gold, refined in the furnaces of life:
or perhaps, so that afterward the stubborn one should
    render punishments   (446)
in the setting of matter aflame, when fiery shall be the
    retribution,
and when those who aforetime had submitted to his
    service
95   shall be tormented exceedingly, since this is what the father of
    evil pays.

These things, then, the Spirit has taught me concerning the
    glory of the angels,
both the first kind and the last. But the measure you may find
    here, too.
The measure is God. However much one approaches the Lord,
so much is one a light, and as one's light is, so much is one's
    boast.

On the Soul

Poem 1.1.8, De anima (PG 37:446–456)

The soul is a breath of God, and has suffered a mixture
of heavenly and earthly, a light hidden in a cave,
but, all the same, divine and imperishable. For it would   (447)
    not be right
for the great God's image to disintegrate in formlessness,
5 like mindless lizards and kine,
even though sin has brought it to a mortal condition.
It is not a consuming fire by nature: for it would not be right
for the eater to be the anima of the eaten; nor an exhalation
or inhalation of air, never standing still;
10 it is not a bloody stream that courses through the flesh,
nor again a harmony of bodily elements, converging into one.
For bodies and an immortal form do not possess
one nature. And what is there in the noble that is not in the
    worst, seeing as a mixture has fashioned them as bad or
    good?
15 And why is there no rational nature in beasts? For a harmony
of form and of mortal flesh is found also in beasts,   (448)
and so the best of them are all "well-tempered," as the saying
    goes.
So much for these views. And here's their rationale: that, since
    the soul
leaves the body when these are absent, soul, they say, must be
    these things.

20 But soul has never been your food, without which no mortal
        thing
    can conceivably live, since energy derives from nourishment.
    I know, again, another explanation, which I myself have never
        accepted,
    for there is no common soul portioned between me and
        everyone else, and
    drifting through the air. In that case, one who inhaled and
25 another who exhaled would be the same in all respects; thus
        everyone
    who lives by breathing would be emptied into everyone else,
    were the soul, in fact, of the nature of air, flowing from one
        person to another.
    But if it resides somewhere, what held it, or what was that
        animal then   (449)
    in my mother's womb, if, when I was outside, she drew
        me in?
30 And if you suppose a mother to have yet more children,
    you honor her with all the more souls gobbled up.
    This kind of talk, insipid triflings of books, is not from
        sensible people;
    likewise with those who make the soul out to be passed
        along
    from body to body, as befits its former lives, whether
        good or wicked,
35 having either honor for virtue, or penalty for some crime;
    and, as if it were a man sloppily putting on clothes
    and taking them off again, struggling uselessly,
    they carry Ixion (a prime scoundrel) about in circles,
        making him
    a beast, a plant, a man, a bird, a snake, a dog, a fish,
40 and often each thing twice, since the circle prescribes it.
    How far then? I have never beheld a wise beast's
        rationality,   (450)

neither a talking shrub. Always a crow's good for cawing,
and always a fish is silent when swimming through watery
    brine.
Again, if there's a final retribution for the soul, as these
    themselves
45 assert, this tenet of theirs is useless. If it's disembodied,
that were quite extraordinary. But if it has a body,
which among the multitude it had will you commit to the fire?
And what is most extraordinary, since you've tied me to many
bodies, and the bond has put me in acquaintance with many,
50 is, How has this alone escaped my notice, what skin it was that
    held me
previously? Which one will do so next? How many have I died
    in? For it has not
grown rich with souls, as with money-bags, this bond of mine.
    But of course,
this too results from protracted wandering, that I should
    suffer amnesia touching my former life.
But hear our doctrine on the soul: it is the best.   (451)
And, drawing from this, we will mix in a bit of pleasure
    with our song.
55 A "when" was, and it then was that the mind's high Word fixed
    fast the world
that formerly was not, at the bidding of the mighty Father's
    mind.
He spoke, and just what he wanted was accomplished. And
    when everything,
the earth, and the sky, and the sea, made up a world,
he sought, again, for one who'd discern his wisdom, mother of
    all things,
60 and to be, for things on earth, a king in divine likeness; and he
    said this:
"My servants, pure and ever-living, hallowed minds, the
    worthy angels,

occupy already the wide heaven,
singers who hymn my praise unceasingly;
but the earth still vaunts in mindless animals.
65   Wherefore it pleases me to form a species
out of both, midway between mortals and immortals:
     thinking man,   (452)
who shall delight in my works, and be a level-headed
     initiate
of heavenly mysteries, and a great power on earth, another
     angel
sprung from the soil, the chanter of my mind and dispositions."
70   Having said this, then, he took up a portion of new-formed
     earth
and with immortal hands set up my shape,
to which he then imparted his own life. For into it he shot
spirit, an efflux of the unseen Godhead.
And from dirt and breath he made a man, image of
75   the immortal: for mind's lordly nature is in both.
And so I feel attachment to this life, through what's earth in
     me,
but inwardly long for another, through the part that's divine.
Such was the conjoining of the original man. Since then,
     however,
bodies derive from flesh, and the soul is mixed in   (453)
     imperceptibly,
80   falling from without into the molding of dust. He who mixes
     them
knows how he first breathed in, and fastened his image to
     earth;
unless someone, coming to the aid of my words, and following
after others, should boldly add this doctrine:
that the first body, after it was blended with us from the soil,
85   later became the human stream, and never leaves off

producing from time to time new human beings from the first-
    formed root;
and the soul breathed out from God thereafter
enters newborn into human patterns,
having out of the first seed been partitioned into many,
90 though keeping an ever-constant form in mortal parts.
Therefore it inherits a governing intellect. But, as on tiny
    pipes,
a great breath blows both pure and squeaky notes,
even though the musician be most talented, while, when (454)
    broader pipes
have come to him, he lets a more professional sound pour
    forth:
95 so it is with a weak soul in weak members:
when these grow strong, it starts to glow, and manifests all the
    mind.
But when the imperishable Son had made for himself a man,
in order to have new glory, and so that, in the last days,
leaving the earth, man might journey from here to God, as
    god,
100 he neither left him at liberty, nor utterly
bound him. But he placed a law in his nature, and engraved
    good things
in his heart, and set him, thus, in the vales of an ever-verdant
paradise, evenly balanced, observing which direction he'd
    incline.
Naked he was, without the form of evil and duplicity.
105 And, as for paradise, it is the heavenly life, it seems to me.
So this is where he placed him, to be a farmer, cultivating his
    words.
He kept from him one plant, a more perfect one,   (455)
having within it a perfect discrimination between good
and evil. For what's perfect is suited for grown-ups,
110 but not for beginners; since this would be as hard to take

as were some very powerful dish to infants.
But when, through the envious murderer's wrestlings,
won over through the female reason's coaxings,
he tasted prematurely the luscious fruit,
115 he clothed his heavy flesh in coats of skin,
as one that bare a corpse (for Christ gorged sin with death),
and out he went from the garden, to the earth that bore him,
receiving a vexatious life. For this cause, God stationed
his fiery zeal for his well-prized plant, as a deadbolt,
120 lest Adam should return too soon to where he was before, (456)
        still ignorant how to avoid a sweet slip's eating aliment,
    and should turn bad, because of the fruit of life. But as in
        wintry
    gales, a seaworthy ship veers round and heads for shore,
    while, again, in fairer winds it either spreads its sails out wide,
125 or sets upon its way by rowers' labors:
    so we, being so far fallen from the great God,
    cannot make our dear return voyage without a struggle.
    So great was the new-sown ruin that from the forefather came
    to miserable humanity; and out of it has sprung a bumper crop.

On the Two Covenants, and the Appearing of Christ

Poem 1.1.9, De Testamentis et Adventu Christi (PG 37:456–464)

[Additamentum (vv. 60, intra v. 18 et v. 19), ed. B. Wyss, in Phyllobolia für P. von der Mühil, Basel, 1946, pp. 160–163.]

Come then, and inquire into the reason for the twofold
    law.
Both an old law and a new have been revealed,   (457)
first to the Hebrews, since even they knew first
the high-ruling God, then afterward to the earth's
    extremities.
5 For God does not guide men with fractious teachings,
like someone inexperienced, since the Word is expert in all
    things,
nor with vacillating ones, which even among mortals is
    disgraceful.
But, as to the loving God's assistance, my account of it goes
    like this:
When the frenzied one had cast the first Adam out of
    paradise
10 by stealing the pestilent fruit of a death-dealing plant,
like an annihilating guide who basely wounds an army,
he sought to do his children evil, too, and plant their doom.
So, breaking them away from the heavenly God by
    underhanded counsel,
he turned the two eyes of man towards the starry heaven,

15   abounding in objects of resplendent beauty, and towards
     the figures   (458)
  of mortal beings, whichever a lust had molded, and a
     myth paid homage to,
  making men to trust in things pernicious to themselves: an
     incorrigible liar,
  growing ever worse as the years went by.

L   But, as often as men did address God, they did so with
     inanities: p.161
  as even faithful Aaron did, for the empty-headed people,
  when, out of the fire's midst, he produced a calf, as a proof of
     hybris;
  or again, as another fabricated another new god for mortals,

5   a figment of the mind—and so the wicked art attended it,
  and wealth that gloats in evil, and time confirmed the
     shame,
  multiplying figurines and sacrifices and feasts—
  a few did smash them, whose mind was their defender,
  who did not call these the God whom not one mind had
     seen,

10   but most people had been shackled, following their own
     eyes.
  Now, so long as evil had a short course, while again (in my
     view)
  an unwritten, inner law served as guide,
  the distinction between good and evil was self-taught.
  But when both the seas and the wide borders of the earth

15   were full of presumption, and slime boiled over with
     arrogance,
  and his creature had already undergone many a
     humbling lesson   p.162
  in tongues divided, floods, and showers of fire,
  yet still did not desire to shake off the chains of its first
     wickedness,

but was held in ever stronger bonds of flesh,
20   hankering after lecheries, bloodshed, and idols:
then it was (this, from the Counselor's word, is most
      amazing)
that, in the hands of Moses his esteemed servant,
God showed his people the way out of Egypt
with mighty wonders, and all the nations were shaken.
25   He led them, going before them in a pillar of fire,
while, from the cloud, he drew them through the chartless
      wilderness.
And when (most marvelous wonder!) he descended from
      heaven
upon the desert mountains, in the depths of the holy cloud,
conversing with his most holy servant, alone with the lone,
30   restraining the crowd with lightning and trumpets and
      quakings—
then he gave the law; and he inscribed it upon tables,
    on either side,
both hidden and open, as much as the stubborn people could
      endure,
so that he might cut them off from the Gentiles, and their
      worst customs.
And just as a father, by easy exercises, straightens the
35   newly-formed ankle of his child's tender foot,
first raising it up a little off the ground,   p.163
prattering sweet things and giving his eyes encouragement,
but then holds back, and, by drawing him on step by step,
he leads the child forward both to run and walk in
      confidence:
40   so likewise Christ the King, taking care of imbecile man,
first cast idols far aside, intending to do the same
with burnt offerings: nevertheless he let these be, while he
      placed within a law

to mitigate wickedness; but finally, neither did these
    sacrifices
remain, but they withdrew, once the people had been broken
    in.
45 And the law, as an overseer for an inheritance, kept me
for the great Father's Child; but when the Child's time drew
    nigh
it willingly withdrew, and the finest Son received his
    inheritance.
This is how God does things. For his custom is to persuade,
    not to manhandle
mortal men. What's forced has no reward, it seems to me.
50 And in fact, when someone comes to the rescue against
    passions, he does not
attack them always with painful things alone, but gives one
    cure
for desire, another for misery, looking in kindness to save the
    one who struggles,
concocting better remedies by the pleasant counsels of art.
And as, when a temple builder raises in the air a rotunda
55 made of stone, with sculpted blocks supporting one
    another,
he first undergirds it with buttresses, and only thereafter
brings stones down from above, and rolls out circle on circle;
but, when these are joined, he casts the buttresses away,
and the circle is firm, surrounded only by thin air:
in the same way, the law was a buttress for a more perfect law.
But the holy Hebrews' destructive brood would not give in
20 to the prophets' laments and entreaties, forever
foreshowing them the anger of the Lord. Rather, indeed, they
    slew them.
Neither did the kings fear, but, so it seems, they too
were evil, by and large, and would not wholly give up their
    groves

and high places, and the bloodthirsty demons.
25   For this reason, they too drew down the mighty God's hot
        wrath,
     and he shook them out. But I, in truth, have come in upon
     this path in place of them, drawing them by a guidance   (459)
        of emulation,
     to bring them back to holiness of faith in Christ,
     when at length, having had their fill of grief, they should turn
        about,
30   for envy of the new-come people, for whom they were
        exchanged.
     These things, however, are for later. Since, then, they dis-
        honored the law,
     they were the last human tribe to be allotted this honor,
     by the eternal Father's will, and his Child's enactments.
     But, seeing as Christ had set in the human body a piece of
        heaven,
35   when he saw it blasted with heart-gnawing evil,
     and the twisted dragon lording it over men,
     he did not, to raise again his portion, send yet
     other aids to treat the disease (for a little cure
     is inadequate against great illnesses); but, emptying himself
40   of his glory as the immortal God the Father's motherless
        Son,
     he appeared for me himself, without a father, a strange
        son;   (460)
     yet no stranger, since from my own kind came this immortal,
        being made
     man by a virgin mother, so that the whole of him might save
        the whole of me.
     For it was, again, the total Adam who fell, through that illicit
        taste.
45   Therefore, humanly, and not after human custom,
     in the hallowed womb of a maid inviolate

he took flesh (amazing! to washed-out minds incredible!)
and came, both God and man, two natures gathered into one:
one hidden, the other open to mankind;
50 of these, the one is God, the latter was created later with us.
He is one God out of both, since the human is mixed with the
        Godhead,
and, because of the Godhead, exists as Lord and Christ.
It is as though another, new Adam, appearing to those on
        earth,
and cloaked round with a shawl, should heal the former one
55 (for I could not draw nigh, because of my passions),   (461)
and trip up unexpectedly the seeming-wise snake
who, approaching this Adam, met up with God,
thinking to carry him off through the force of his wickedness,
like the ocean that breaks on a hard and jagged rock.
60 When he appeared, both earth and heaven shook
about the birth. The heavenly choir sent down hymns;
the star from the East led the Magi on their way,
bearing gifts in worship of the newborn King.
This is my teaching concerning Christ's novel birth.
65 Nothing was shameful there, since sin alone is shameful:
therefore was nothing shameful, since the Word
        established it.
Neither by man's seed did he become man, but it was   (462)
        from that flesh
that the Spirit had hallowed beforehand, of an unwedded,
        cherished mother
that he came, a self-made man; and he was purified for my
        sake.
70 For he accepted everything, even paying the law an offering of
        thanks,
or else giving it a send-off in its retirement, as I suppose.
But after he was proclaimed by the clear-shining
        beacon of a

great light forerunning the Child, forerunning the gospel,
heralding Christ my God in the midst of the desert—
75 he appeared, he came as the mid-point of the peoples, both the
       far-off
   and the near (for he is the common Cornerstone for both of
       them);
   and he granted to mortals a double purification,
   that of the Spirit, ever-flowing, who has cleansed my former
       evil
   born with the flesh, and that of our blood.
80 For this, too, is mine, this blood that Christ my God   (463)
       poured out
   in restitution for ancient longings, and as a ransom for the
       world.
   If then I were someone invincible, not a man easily turned,
   I would have needed only the great God's one commandment,
   which would have cared for me, saved me, and raised me to
       great honor.
85 But now, since God did not make me a god, but fashioned me
   inclinable both ways, and slanted, he therefore supports me,
       along with many others,
   who possess one grace of the Baptism given to men. For, as
       once
   the Hebrew children escaped destruction by an anointing of
       blood
   that cleansed their doorposts, when in a single night all the
       firstborn
90 of the Egyptian people perished: so for me, too, is this washing
   a seal of the God who wards off evil—for little children   (464)
       it is
   a seal, for grown-ups, again, it is a cure and the finest seal,
   divinely flowing from Christ the giver of light: so that, fleeing
   the depth of anguish and lifting up the neck lightly from under
       its burden,

95 I might turn my two feet back again towards life. For a traveler,
        too,
     refreshed from toil, rouses his knees again with renewed vigor.
     Common to us all is the air, and the earth is common, too.
     Common is the heaven so wide, whose circuit revolves the
        seasons.
     Common to humanity is the Baptism that saves man.

On Providence

Poem 1.1.6, De eodem argumento (PG 37:430–438)

Away with them, those who deny what is divine,   (430)
and ascribe no cause to the good, ineffable
composition of the universe,
whether in creation or in the upkeep of all things.
5 Away with them! who acknowledge a swarm of deities,
or a potency of demons, good and evil.
Away with the deniers of Providence
who, as though afraid of being saved by God,
either assign the universe to an erratic "swoosh!"
10 or else credit it to the movements of stars.
And how, and whence, and by whom are these moved?
If it's by God, how can that be first, which God turns
    round?   (431)
For it belongs to the weaver, and it's his to weave it anew.
But, if it's not from God, how is it to stand up out of
    anarchy,
15 or again, from battling with one stronger? And why
    no battle?
For, take away Providence, and you take up arms
    against God.
Unless you'd make God, too, subject to fate,
unwillingly bearing the tyranny of his own weaving.
In this way these are caught by their own words.
20 For us, rather, there's one God who guides this universe,
wisely revolving and forming it, as he wills,

by his own very words and inclinations,
even if it seems not all things turn aright.
Yes, many there are, among the wisest even, who've been
    troubled
25 by reason of things' inequity, both now and formerly.
What need is there to mention all of them? Consider
    with me
David, what he suffered. Seeing the wicked prospering   (432)
(as they thought), he was powerfully upset,
lest someone should credit their gains to the nature of their
    business,
30 as though no one at all were set above us.
But he himself knew their undoing. For consider with me,
he says, their common end, what a turnabout!
You've sown seed? From what you've sown, you will see corn
    as well.
But if you don't know the reasons, not so God's Reason.
35 For a painter is not ignorant, because you don't know
    painting,
nor is a geometer as you, if you can't read his symbols.
You've grasped one thing, but follow wisely the other.
For this, too, is reason, to be persuaded by reason.
If everything were obvious, tell me, where would
    be believing?
40 For faith is an unmeddling assent.
But this I also think, perhaps with wisdom:
I have not promised that you will come by things like
    these,   (433)
being rich, carefree, or having bright children,
but goodness of life, and hopes for what's to come,
45 so that, instead of present things, one looks for greater.
How would it be fair, in some transaction,
for you both to covet the goods, and hold on to your money?
Or does this right of all belong only to you?

An amazing appetite, this, and a strange mode of commerce!
50   Either let go of this, friend, or abandon that;
     but, if you really need some basis for your teaching,
     don't go beyond those things that have been rightly
          laid down.
     But why then, you ask, were things this way for the
          people of old?
     Faith then had not as yet been rooted in,   (434)
55   and things down here were a pledge of things of
          the mind,
     just as milk is for infants who are going to be men.
     Now, a proof of this statement. For even then it
          happened that
     the greatest of crimes were in some way forgiven,
     but crimes less great were sorely punished:
60   a backwards linking-up of what's right in each case.
     And there were chastisements for the wise that went
          beyond measure.
     Let David convince you of these things, and Moses,
     Elisha too, remembering whom, I shudder.
     For of these, one was chastised lightly for his sins;
65   while another, who'd even been granted the vision
          of God,
     who both received the Law, and led out to safety so
          great a host: (435)
     for a slight offence, which was even for the children's sake,
     he received in return so huge a blow against his hope.
     So shadowy was the Law itself back then.
70   So purification was through victims' blood,
     and feeble sprinklings of unhallowed bodies.
     In this way, the best thing was to escape from something
          worse
     if in fact nothing better were at hand, while, with little rules,
     religion was circumscribed for the people of that time.

75 Should I tell of something yet greater? Let it be said.
    They never had such an offering as
    we do, by God's sufferings,
    and by the Lamb who was slain by reason of my vices.   (436)
    So then, this offering was greater than theirs: and,
        if greater,
80 admit that they had a greater need of toils,
    while we've less need, who've met with greater blessings.
    And first, before all else, this must be said:
    do not overly praise a life of prosperity,
    you who can think of greater than visible things;
85 lest maybe the high road, hard to travel, shall be mine,
    while you take the easy way, circled round with
        mountains.
    My hardship is preferable to your ease.
    Sometime you've observed a stout bull in the stable,
    stirred up, gleaming with bodily health,
90 baring the neck, and bending down the head;   (437)
    another shriveled, bad-faced on account of farming;
    later, the one's appointed for the butcher,
    while the other feeds both himself and his master.
    Which do you think is the luckier of these two?
95 Isn't it the slim one, worn down by a yoke?
    Plainly so. But you desire bigness,
    even if evil, and linked with what is evil.
    Or do you recommend a water-bearer's load?
    Or does someone struck in the head seem to you strong?
100 And is pleasure utterly a saving medicine?
    Oftentimes many are saved by what is bitter.
    But pleasure leads, by and large, to what is worse.
    Does not a son respect his father's rod,
    if he has any sense? But, as for him who thinks such
        kindness evil,
105 he is no son, nor does a rod reprove him.   (438)

So then, what if you strive for a crown, like Job?
Give praise for these things in yourself, and you'll find it easier,
making an exhortation for your hardship,
and earning hope by thanksgiving.
110 For it's a wicked servant who makes a joke
of honoring his master; and when he is beaten, he thinks that
    he is wronged.
It is necessary to accept every turn of the rudder
by which God leads me out from both struggle and storm,
till he has harbored me in a fair haven:
115 if indeed he did not build the vessel to no purpose,
but towards a good and well-intentioned end.

Against Apollinarius

Poem 1.1.10, De Incarnatione, adversus Apollinarium
(PG 37:464–470)

The most great Mind, we know, was fastened into
all the nature of man, consisting of three things,　　　　　(465)
soul, mind, and the body's mass,
the whole former Adam, save for sin.
5　For when he had come to be the God-man,
God came to an end as man, to honor me,
so that, by the very things he took on, he might restore,
and destroy sin's accusation utterly,
and, by dying, slaughter the slaughterer.
10　He is God: from above, simple; then, fastened together;
afterward, fastened up by God-murdering hands.　　　　(466)
This is the doctrine of the God who's been mingled
　　　with you.
He was God from on high, coeternal with the Father,
both divine Word and Maker of all things,
15　superior to time and passions and body.
But when, by the tree of knowledge, the envious one smote us
and had laid waste all our nature
as an easy catch, subject to condemnation:
then, so as to break the envious one's pride,
20　and create anew the rotted image,　　　　　　　　　(467)
God came to be among us. For, through a holy virgin,
God was conceived and was born.
He is wholly God and man, saving me wholly,

the Son both known by mind and seen by sight.
25   According to you, I'm a man-worshipper, since I revere
the whole Word mystically united with us,
who, as Savior, is both God and man.
You, then, are a flesh-worshipper, since you present me as
        mindless,
if I may creditably return your gibe.
30   Either allow this, sir, or drop your allegation,
if, that is, you wish to be a fair arbiter of debate.
If God for you is what from God is inferior
(for flesh is much inferior to what is after the image),
for me, he is also what is better: for mind is closer
        to God.
35   But you have the nerve to speak of a semi-human: (468)
for what has not been assumed does not get saved.
What do you say, O most wise sentinel of the Word,
who have been vexed at those who divide the divinity:
don't you also divide God's constitution,
40   giving him this of mine, and then not that,
mixing in flesh, but shaving away the mind,
as though you were concerned you might be standing as one
        whole?
How then shall a one encompass two totalities,
as though we might be worried the skin would break?
45   What nonsense! A single soul has received both mind
and reason; but where then for you is the great
mind, when God is there? If the flesh is mindless,
I have been deceived. The skin is mine; whose is the soul?
What is God's nativity from the Virgin?
50   How did a nature of diversities come together in one?   (469)
This is something ineffable, I perceive, when,
with a tiny reason, I seek to measure things exceeding reason.
The purifying Spirit came upon a virgin
within whom the Word was formed into a man,

55   the total price of redemption for the total mortal man.
     And, seeing as God has no admixture of flesh,
     while soul and mind stand, as it were, in middle ground,
     the flesh, then, is both God's housemate and his icon:
     God's nature mingles with what is akin to it,
60   and from there has communion also with the flesh.
     Thus, both what deifies and what is deified are the one same God.
     What then was the outcome, on each hand? I'd say this:
     that the one was blended with flesh, while the other, being flesh,
     participated in all that is mine, save the passions of sin.   (470)
65   Shall I ask to whom went the blood that Christ shed forth?
     If to the wicked one—alas, Christ's blood for him who is evil!
     But if to God—why, when we were under another's power?
     For it's always to one who holds power that a ransom is paid.
     The truth is this: he offered himself to God,
70   so as to snatch us from him who had us in his power,
     so that, in exchange for him who fell, he might take
     the Christ: but he who christens cannot be caught.
     This is our opinion. We respect, however, the typologies.
     The sum of it is this: worship the Trinity.

On the Incarnation of Christ

Poem 1.1.11, De Christi Incarnatione (PG 37:470–471)

Foolish is he or she who does not worship the ever-existing
Word of God, the Lord, as equally God with the supernal
    Father.
Foolish is he or she who does not worship the Word,
    the Lord,   (471)
a human here appearing, as equally God with the heavenly
    Word.
5 The one divides the Word from the great Father, the other
our human form and fleshiness from the Word.
Though being God, the Father's Word took on our human
    being,
to mingle it with God, and be little amongst earthlings.
He is one God out of both, being so human as to make me
10 God, instead of human. Be merciful, O wounded one on high!
Let that much suffice you. What more have I to do with an
    ineffable mind and mixture?
Both are God, you mortals, be content with reason's limits.
If, then, I've won you over, much the better. But if you blacken
the page with many myriads of words,
15 come, and I'll inscribe these little verses upon tables
with letters from my carving pen, which have no blackness in
    them.

Concerning the Genuine Books of Scripture

Poem 1.1.12, De veris Scripturae libris (PG 37:471–474)

Always be revolving, in speech and in your mind,
upon the words of God: for God gave this
to be a prize for labors, a little light for seeing
5   something hidden; or else, to be a blessing,
that by the holy God's great laws you might be pierced;
or, third, that by these cares you might withdraw your mind
    from earthly things.
But, lest you be stolen in mind by foreign books
(for in them many evil things have been inserted)
receive, friend, this list of mine of books that are approved.
    There are, in all, twelve historical books
10   of the older, Hebrew wisdom.
First, Genesis, then Exodus, and Leviticus,   (473)
Numbers, then Deuteronomy.
After that, Joshua and Judges. Ruth is eighth,
while the ninth and tenth books are the Acts of the Kings,
15   then Chronicles. Lastly you have Ezra.
And there are five poetic books: first Job;
next, David; then three that come from Solomon:
Ecclesiastes, the Song, and Proverbs.
Likewise there are five books from the prophetic Spirit.
20   In one writing are contained the Twelve:
Hosea and Amos, and Micah the third,
then Joel, Jonah, Obadiah,

and Nahum, Habbakuk, and Zephaniah,
Haggai, Zechariah, and Malachi.
25   These, then, are one book. The second is Isaiah.
Then Jeremiah, he who was called from the womb.   (474)
Then Ezekiel, and Daniel's grace.
Thus, I have laid down two and twenty ancient volumes,
corresponding to the Hebrews' letters.
30   Now then, count also the number of the New Mystery.
Matthew wrote Christ's miracles to the Hebrews;
Mark wrote to Italy, and Luke to Greece;
to all wrote John, the great herald, he who penetrated heaven.
Next comes the Acts of the wise Apostles.
35   And there are ten epistles of Paul,
and seven catholic epistles, of which one is by James,
two by Peter, three of John again,
and Jude's is the eighth. There you have all of them.
If there is anything else besides these, it is not among the
     genuine.

Another Prayer for a Safe Journey

Poem 1.1.37, Alia de prospero itinere precatio (PG 37:520–521)

Not a step is lifted without you,
Christ the Lord, who to your own human kind
are all good things, and, in everything, have fashioned a right
    way.
Trusting in you, I too keep to this path; but escort me
5   uninjured, and ferry all the things my heart has sought,
and, Lord, lead me back again to my humble home
where, night and day, I may supplicate you freely.

In Praise of Virginity

Poem 1.2.1, In laudem virginitatis (PG 37:521–578)

Let us wreathe Virginity in our garlands,
singing from clear hearts in clearest hymns.
For this is the choicest offering of our life,
brighter than gold or amber or ivory: (522)
5   by these things, virgin desire casts down pedestrian life,
flying on wings of mind towards the high-ruling God.
And, as the song begins, let those who are pure come join in
    the praises:
for the gift of song is common to all who are
    blameless.
But let the malevolent muzzle their ears with doors;   (523)
10 but if any would open them, let them hallow their mind
    by the poem.
Hail, Virginity! gift of God, giver of blessings,
mother of innocence, Christ's portion, yokemate of
the heavenly, unyoked beauties: for unwedded are,
first, God, secondly God's ever-existing choir.
15 And he is the fountain of lights, the light that can be
    neither
named nor grasped, who flees from an intellect swiftly
    drawing near,
forever outpacing the wits of all, so that, longing,
we might be drawn ever newly higher. Those, in turn, are

secondary lights, holding from the Trinity a royal boast.

20 The original Virgin is the Holy Trinity. From the beginningless
Father is the Lord the Son—not that the Father is moved by
anything outside him
(for he is to all things the Way and Root and Beginning), (524)
nor that he begets a Child in a way akin to mortals,
but as light comes forth from light. But from the Child

25 there is no other well-loved Child, claiming a similar boast:
so that the one remains the sole Parent, while the other is
sole Son and most Unique from the Unique; these come together in one
with the great Spirit, who likewise comes from the Father,
one God opening up in threefold lights.

30 Such then is the Trinity's pure nature. And from it are
the angels, dazzling, invisible, who go therefore about
the great throne, since they are nimble intelligences,
fire and divine spirits coursing swiftly through the air,
hurriedly attending to his great behests.

35 For these there is no marriage, pains, or worries, (525)
neither the fierce, outrageous battle of the passions;
they are not divided
into members, or by houses: of one mind with one
another,
and each one with himself. One nature, one intellect,
one same desire for the mighty Lord God. They do not take
pleasure

40 in children or wives, being busied with a sweet pain;
wealth is not dear to them, nor those many cares of evil
that the earth bears to mortals. They do not plow,
nor do they ply the sea for the incorrigible stomach's sake,
the stomach, chief of evils; they have in common that one best
food,

45   to feed on the great God's word, and to draw from
        the brilliant Trinity a boundless light. They live a
              single life
        as the pure servants of the pure God,
        simple, noetic, translucent, not coming from bodies   (526)
        (for bodies, being compounds, are again destroyed),
50   nor entering upon bodies, but remaining just what they
              were originally.
        With these is godlike Virginity, a ready way
        to God, following close to the Immortal One's reasons
        as he wisely steers the rudder of the great world;
        which also is found in the heavenly, earthly, magnificent,
              mortal,
55   holy, suffering human race, the Lord's prize possession.
        Come, then, and I will speak of the beloved mysteries
              of God,
        whatever Virginity has revealed in these last times.
        Once it was, when black night concealed all things.
        There was then no beloved morning light; nor had the sun
60   made its fiery way from the east.
        The crescent moon, night's glory, did not show.
        But all things were jumbled with each other, uselessly   (527)
              wandering
        locked together in the murky chains of firstborn chaos.
        But you, O blessed Christ, obedient to the counsels of
65   the great Father, distinguished all things beautifully
              throughout the world.
        Now indeed the original light appeared, so that all
              his works
        might rejoice, being full of light. Then, after this,
        heeled around the starry heaven, O marvelous wonder!
        illumined by the sun and the moon. He spoke to these,
70   telling the firstborn to shine upon men

with streams of a boundless light, and revolve the hours,
to the other, that it should brighten the darkness, and give a
    second day.
Then he set under the earth my foundation, and locked
    the sea
in the earth's arms, and in the sea the earth,
75   the ocean's inlets flowing round about it. In this way,
    all was
a world, both earth, and heaven, and the sea,   (528)
the heaven adorned with heavenly lights,
the sea with things that swim, and the dry land with
    terrestrials.
The Father, then, beholding and knowing all this
    arrangement,
80   was pleased in the likeminded works of his Son, the Lord.
He sought also for one to understand his wisdom, mother
    of all things,
and to be, for things on earth, a king in divine likeness; and he
    said this:
"My servants, pure and ever-living, the worthy angels,
occupy already the wide heaven: blessed minds,
85   hymners chanting my praise unceasingly;
but the earth still vaunts in mindless animals.
So it pleases me to form a mixed species, out of both,
between mortals and immortals, thinking man,
who should rejoice in my works, and be a level-headed   (529)
    initiate
90   in heavenly mysteries, and a great power upon earth,
    another angel
sprung from the soil, the chanter of my mind and
    dispositions."
Having said this, he took a piece of new-formed earth
and with immortal hands set up my shape.

To it, then, he gave a portion of his own life. For into it he shot
95 spirit, an efflux of the unseen Godhead.
And from dirt and breath he made a man, image of the
immortal: for mind's lordly nature is in both.
Therefore I have an affection for this life, through what's earth
        in me,
but inwardly long for another, through the part that's
        divine.
100 But when the divine-terrestrial creature had appeared   (530)
        upon earth
in the vales of an ever-verdant garden,
he had as yet no suitable helper for his life.
Then came this greatest marvel of the all-wise Word:
taking that man whom he'd formed as a spectator of
        his world,
105 and parting in twain my root, and the seed of
multiform life, by his great life-giving hand,
he removed from his side a sole rib, and built it into
a woman, and, mixing in desire in their breast,
he set them both loose to embrace each other;
110 not always, however, nor with everyone, but he set a limit to
        their desires,
that which they call marriage, a rein for matter's want of
        measure:
so that people should not go panting and raging   (531)
        uncontrollably
after each other hotly like cattle
and break away the holy human race from the love
115 of celibacy, raising up wars and hatreds for all people,
an overpowering madness for unguided fools.
Since then mother earth was deficient in human beings,
thus lacking that highest ornament that was meant for her,
while, moreover, the first created man, by his iniquities

120 and by the envy of the bitter serpent, was expelled
      from paradise by the wicked taste of the murderous plant,
      being weighed down to his earth in coats of skins:
      therefore what was best for human beings was a coupling
      and marriage, the nature of human generation, a defense
            against destruction,
125 so that, in those who pass away and in those who are   (532)
            born thereafter,
      the changing human race might be drawn on like a river,
      being impermanent through death, but permanent through
            its children.
      But when both the sea and the wide borders of the earth,
      both east and west, the north side and the south,
130 were full of people, and the slime bubbled over with
            arrogance,
      and his creature had already undergone many a humbling
            lesson
      in tongues divided, floods, and showers of fire,
      and in teachings by the written law, and by prophets,
      yet still did not desire to shake off the chains of its first
            wickedness,
135 but was held in ever stronger bonds of flesh,
      hankering after lecheries, bloodshed, and idols:
      finally, the human race inherited this honor   (533)
      by the immortal Father's decree, and the Child's
            enactments.
      Seeing as Christ had set in the human body a piece
            of heaven,
140 when he saw it blasted with heart-gnawing evil,
      and the twisted dragon lording it over men,
      he did not, to raise again his portion, send yet
      other aids to treat the disease (for a little cure
      is inadequate against great illnesses); but, emptying himself

145   of his heavenly glory as the unchangeable Image of
      the heavenly One, both humanly and not after human custom,
      in the hallowed womb of a maid inviolate
      he took flesh (amazing! to washed-out minds incredible!)
      and came, both God and man, two natures gathered
            into one:
150   one hidden, the other open to mankind;   (534)
      of these, the one is God, the latter was created later with us,
      at that time when, in the womb, God was mingled with things
            human.
      He is one God out of both, since the human is mixed with the
            Godhead,
      and, because of the Godhead, exists as Lord and Christ.
155   This was the second mixture, since the first one had been
            contemned.
      First I received a share in the divine breath, then later
      Christ took on both my soul and all my members,
      that earlier, free Adam, who was naked
      of sin, before he had seen the serpent, and had tasted of the
            fruit
160   and of death, who nourished his spirit upon simple
      heavenly ideas, as a radiant mystic of God and divine
            things.   (535)
      Recreating this Adam, God came into human nature,
      so that, by contending, and by triumphing over death
      by death, and over the taste by gall, and the lawless hands
165   by the nails, and the tree by the cross, and earth by being
            uplifted,
      he might raise up Adam again towards life and honor.
      And, having purified through sufferings his holy body, that
            body that he gathered together
      from the ends of the earth into a man, and united into one
            human being,

and placed in the embracing arms of the great Godhead:
170 by the blood of the Lamb he cleanses from every defilement,
lifting away guilt from mortals by a heavenly method.
O Lord, who is able to search out your mind and depth,
who can count the drops of rain, or the sand of the sea,
or who knows the pathways of the wind?
175 But who, again, can comprehend the traces of your will,   (536)
    O Blessed One,
  you who rule on high, observing all things and governing
    all things,
  whatsoever boundless eternity conceals? But when the human
    mind
  stretches toward you, it perceives a glimpse of light, like
    swiftest lightning
  fleeing through the air. Nevertheless, O True One,
180 when you transported man from here by your sufferings
  you placed him in another life, one that is free instead
    of evil.
  Formerly, life and the world were in travail towards the earth,
  and a multitude of people attended the king of the denizens of
    earth:
  those whom he had snatched from the great King by
    covetousness.
185 But now that Christ has delivered them out of the hand of dire
    evil,
  he leads them back again to the great Lord and a better world.
  The former of these human states is marriage, the latter,
    divine unweddedness;   (537)
  the former is that of earth, the latter, that of the heavenly
    choir.
  As when a man inscribes lifeless images on a drawing board,
190 he makes a first draft, sketching out the form in
  faint and indistinct lines; then afterward
  he finishes the whole form with many and various colors:

in the same way, virginity, the eternal Christ's inheritance,
first appeared in only a few people, and obscurely;
195 while the Law ruled, it was visible in indistinct colors,
and its hidden radiance illuminated only a few.
But when Christ came by way of a holy Virgin
Mother, being himself unyoked, divine in form, spotless
(since it was needful that he should come to be apart from
    marriage and a father),
200 he hallowed womankind, and shook off bitter Eve,
and he dismissed the laws of the flesh, with mighty words (538)
the letter gave way to the spirit, and grace came in the
    midst;
then, truly, radiant Virginity illuminated mankind,
both liberated from and liberating the feeble world,
205 being so far superior to the married life, the life of bonds,
as soul is superior to flesh,
and the wide, unchanging heaven of the blessed ones is to the
    changing life of earth,
as far as God is better than man.
And the blameless choir stands around the light-bearing
    Lord,
210 heavenly, hastening from earth to become God,
Christ-bearing, serving the Cross, scorning the world,
dead to earthly things, caring only for things of heaven,
being beacons of the world, a translucent mirror of the
    light;
who gaze upon God, while God belongs to them, and
    they to God.
215 Come then, ladies, you who are in agreement with your
    ribs, initiates
of wedlock, who go with head held high and with eyes   (539)
    that strike terror,
wearing gold interspersed with exquisite stones

and luxurious coats upon your dainty limbs:
tell us how many advantages marriage and its yoke provide
220 mortals; afterward we shall call upon the unwedded lot.
These, then, inflated, will speak glibly thus:
Hearken, O beloved children of Marriage, the King of earthly
folk,
to Us, whose preoccupation has been Marriage and the bond
of life,
the bond of the human race, and of our blood,
225 which bond the Child of the immortal Father laid down as an
ordinance,
ever since he bound the first Adam to his rib,
so that, from man and by marriage, there should come a
human fruit,
which, though mortal, should remain sprouting with
children.
Wherefore, honoring this law and beloved wedlock,   (540)
230 we come together in union, since we have come into being
from dust,
in reverence for the most ancient law of dust and God.
For, indeed, all those natures whose portion is the wide
heaven
are unwedded, superior to passions and grievous sorrows;
but, for mortals, marriage and the yoke are profitable.
235 They are the root of beloved saplings and of longed-for fruits
and the worthy support of a life sweet to the mind.
First of all, God is the begetter of all things. (And, O Christ, be
gracious
to your holy laws, more than you were before.)
Love's yoke is on him, since he has also made the earth and air
240 and sea to abound with children, the gifts of marriage.
If in truth the law of desire applies to the date palm also, whose
foliage towers aloft,

such that male and female have intercourse in the   (541)
    season of spring
by gardeners' hands, to make swell a fruit resembling a bunch
    of grapes,
and if, again, a stone is engendered from a pair of small
    stones
245 coming into union, as men versed in geology relate,
then, even for soulless things, there is marriage and the bond
    of love.
But what have I to do with the teachings and longings of
    foreign things?
Behold what blessings sensible marriage has afforded human
    beings.
Who's it that's taught wise friendship, and discovered the
    depths,
250 with all that earth, the sea, and heaven contain?
Who's laid down laws for cities? And, even earlier,
who built the cities, and discovered arts by counsels?
Who's filled the markets, homes, and amphitheaters?
Who's recruited the army in war, and tables at feasts?
255 Who's supplied a choir that harmonizes in the sacrificial
    temple?
Who's freed us from a bestial life, and plowed the earth,   (542)
and taught plants' cultivation, and, on the high seas,
launched a black ship, propelled by the winds?
Who's bound land and sea by a watery path,
260 and joined in one things distant? Who but marriage?
So much, then, for the aforesaid. But what follows is
    better still.
By marriage, we are hands and ears and feet to one another.
And marriage has made the weak one twice as strong,
being a great joy to friends and a sorrow to enemies.
265 And common worries lighten anxiety,

while joys had in common are sweeter for both.
Wealth is made sweeter for those who are likeminded;
while likemindedness is sweeter than both, for those
    in need.
For both of them, the key to wisdom and desires alike
270 is marriage, and the seal of beloved need. (543)
One young colt rejoices the spirit by leapings of love.
One cup, untouched by strangers, of the domestic fountain,
neither flowing outside, nor from outside adducing another:
united in the flesh, likeminded, sharpening
275 in one another, through similar desire, the spur of piety.
Nor does marriage estrange someone from God;
rather, one clings the more to him, since he gives the more
    incentive.
But as a little wind sends forth a little boat,
skimming swiftly along the waves with its sails unfurled,
280 or as hands propel it, urged on by a rower's orders;
a small wind moves not many, but a stronger wind propels
a heavier vessel traveling on the sea:
so also the unmarried, since they live without care,
have less need of help from the mighty God. (544)
285 But he who guards his beloved wife and possessions
and children, cutting his way through the great sea of life,
has a greater need, and God surrounds him the more
    with love.
Such is marriage; but the loveless life is maimed,
unpitied, obscure, heartless, haunting the high hills,
290 it has no remedy for passions, no medicine
for the debility of age; children who begrudge their own
    parents,
providing them no sweet support for life. They have no joy
in gatherings, or festivities; unsmiling; divorced from the
    world,

they have entered upon this life, but they do not love
295 life's roots; their spirit has no sympathy with men.
But if anyone desiring virtue dishonors love,
virtue is not remote from love, not only because
beloved marriage existed for all the pious in times of old, (545)
    but also because from gentle love come births
300 and witnesses of Christ's passions, and prophets,
patriarchs, priests, trophy-bearers, kings,
adorned with every kind of virtue. For the earth did not
    put forth
good people, as some say about the gargantuan tribes
    of giants,
but all are the offspring and boast of marriage.
305 Who pointed out the great ruling God to men,
even those far distant, and filled the mind
with divine love, and guided us to another life?
Who cleansed souls for all folks of renown?
Faithful Enoch was married. So was he who saved
310 the whole world from the waters with a few human souls
    and floating species,
Noah the great. Abraham was father of cities and of
    peoples,   (546)
and bound his son for Christ, as an altar sacrifice.
Moses led the people out of Egypt's oppression
with great miracles, and received the law from on high
315 in tables of stone, and looked straight on at God.
Aaron was a faithful priest among the foremost.
Valiant Joshua delayed the course of moon and sun,
causing his enemies a longer slaughter and sorrow.
And you, blessed one, holy Samuel, bore the horn of oil for
    those who were anointed.
320 David was most celebrated among all kings,
and Solomon had chief renown for wisdom. Nor will I omit

the prophets. A chariot snatched Elijah up to heaven.
And who is not amazed at John, the midpoint between law
    and spirit,
the far-famed Forerunner of the highest Light?
325 Or, again, at the dozen famed disciples who then   (547)
    followed,
or at the vigorous might of Paul, the great-hearted
    explorer of heaven,
and at others who have been, and now are, most excellent,
the pillar of the Word, the world's renown, the people's
    foundations?
All of these marriage and Christ have given to men.
330 Nor again did the women famous for religion
(of whom so many are found in the God-inspired books)
advance without marriage and the good report of the flesh.
I would make yet a grander claim, paying honor to
    my love.
Christ himself was conceived in a pure but human belly,
335 and slipped out from a woman's womb,
thus mixing half of human marriage with divinity.
One thing, beyond all else, is my greatest claim to strength:
    even if the unwedded
should be stronger, these too, in fact, are my race, just like
    everyone else.
For those who have married do not come from the   (548)
    unmarried, but from marriage
340 come the celibate. We urge our children: refrain from the
    contest.
You may not be fathers, but from fathers you have had your
    existence.
Thus far Marriage. Afterward, with downcast visage,
in tattered rags and with weakened senses,
unshod, pining away, her eyes fixed upon the ground,

₅ comes Virginity, opening her lips ever so slightly with
        shame,
    reddening her cheek with her chaste blood,
    and, though she would be hidden, silently drawing the
        covering from her head.
    There and then I would win her over with words like these:
    O child of heaven, and inwardly glorious,
350 O you who stand together with the choirs of those
    who hymn the great Governor, even if the earth and your body
        hold you back,
    come forward and speak your part. And I myself will stand
        before you.
    For indeed, O queen, you came to me once as a gift
        of God,   (549)
    you came to me, but, all the same, come now and be
        propitious still.
355 Who is it that leads me, all unwilling, towards this tribunal?
    And, as I strive to honor my God, by works, by stillness,
    by labors of day and hymns of night,
    by streams of tears and holy purifications,
    who summons me to a vain battle and verbal squabblings?
360 For my strength is not in respect of people, nor am I agile
    with words, nor do I mingle in human concourses, nor exult
    in the votes of favorable judges (only few of them
    take care, and that but little, for right judgment,
    and often they cause the scales of justice to tilt this way or
        that).
365 Let the honors of life be for others. But, as for me,
    I have one law, one intention: filled with love,   (550)
    to wend my way from here, a light-bearer, towards the
        high-ruling God.
    But as for other goods, the desire for them affects my heart but
        little,

such things as vain people dream of, inflated with useless
  vanities,
370 things quickly gained and which perish as rapidly
as smoke or steam, or a flowing breeze,
as sand ever swept about by disturbing winds,
or as the trail of a ship upon the sea.
I would prefer to be dishonored among men
375 and to have a small reputation among the heavenly beings,
  ever-existing,
rather than, possessing all things, to fall short of God.
Nevertheless, I tremble and am afraid, lest somebody,
  lifted up,
plying nimbly in the stratosphere on a new-formed wing of
Virginity,
because of these speeches should most swiftly plummet to the
  earth.
380 For this reason I have entered into the fray, as my
  parents' ally,   (551)
bearing in hand a helping word from God.
To my mother first of all I will speak, as much as is fitting,
you stated and recounted truly,
lovely Marriage, and I agreed (for indeed
385 I will begin where your discourse left off) that marriage
is the root of the unmarried. And in fact, it is both root and
  beginning.
Who would reject the parents of temperate people?
But you didn't tell the whole truth. But receive,
even though you are a mother, a wise and sensible teaching,
390 and a mystery of great wisdom concerning birth
that the hidden places of the great God revealed to me.
A man is not the father of the whole human being, as they say,
but of that which is of flesh and blood, both of which
perish. But the soul is a breath of the mighty God,   (552)

395 falling from without into the molding of dust. He that mixed
        them
     knows how he first breathed in and mixed his image with
        earth.
     And your love testifies to my words. For it is only
        half-perfect:
     it doesn't care about children's souls, but only their bodies;
     when these are sick, you worry, when these bloom with health,
        you rejoice.
400 For father and reverend mother are more pained at heart
     over little disfigurements that come their children's way
     than for great evils and worse disfigurations of their souls.
     For of their bodies they are the parents, but of their souls they
        are not.
     But, if I call you mother, even of the inferior part,
405 why are you jealous if the unmarried have a better father?
     Freely give place, therefore, to the great begetter of
        mankind,
     honoring Virginity, which follows God the Father.   (553)
     So much, then, to my mother; let what has been said up
        to now suffice.
     But, as for me, O beloved children of God the King of all,
410 in honor of this law, I mingled lovely oneness of mind
     towards God alone, and abandoned the desire of dust;
     it was this law that the immortal Father's Child, who was born
        of the unyoked,
     an incorruptible one from him who is unperishing, established
        on high,
     ever since he placed the first Adam in paradise
415 unwedded, then, later, when giving the law, sanctified the
        people,
     and by the law purified those who'd given birth, and honored
        the temple

by the most chaste bodies of the priests, changing in their
    courses.
The great father of John is a witness to this, who did not go to
sire his beloved son, the one he'd been promised in
    the temple,
420 the great Christ's Herald to mortal men,   (554)
not before he'd performed the mysteries to God during
    days of abstinence.
But the end of the law is Christ, who was joined with
    humankind
through a virginal womb, in such a way that marriage should
    decline towards the ground.
And, in point of fact, marriage thus gave way, and a better
    world arose,
425 and death, traveling from the firstborn parent through
    corruptible flesh,
by a flow in those who beget and by birth in those who are
    perishing,
by Virginity was deadened and destroyed, like a mighty wave
on a headland rock, and a flame eaten up by water.
Besides these things, who takes joy in cities and asthenic laws,
430 in markets and commerce, and in competitions
of speeches in honor of youths too soon deceased?
Who praises an army in wartime and tables amidst the
    festivities?
Or who praises swollen-headed skill, whether it lie in   (555)
    one's hands' productions
or, instead, in spiderlike words and weavings,
435 simultaneously brought forth and dissolved into thin air?
Who, then, takes joy in such things, and in the labors of
    gardening,
in the course of a swift-sailing ship, driven by
    pounding winds?

Such things are not taught by marriage, but are a small
        portion
of Adam's ancient punishment, by which things the bitter
        serpent
440 creeps up on me, eyeing my heel. But if they're due to
        marriage,
explain how. For they are not my companions as I press on
from here towards another life, and all such commodities are
        destroyed
today, or with the world's unstable flow.
For, flowing, you pass your way through this life's flux,
445 and, running past things running, barely skim them.   (556)
But if you rejoice in the wise, since from you they came
        into being,
accept, too, the badness of scoundrels, since you're their root
        as well.
You are the root of Cain, and of the Sodomites, and of those
        whom, in their madness,
Christ scattered at the tower, and of those whose hybris a
        heavenly tempest quenched,
450 which simultaneously cleansed all the earth for those who
        breathe.
Who raised ill-meaning Pharaoh, and Ahab's rashness,
and the most bitter kings of the Assyrians? Or who raised
        baleful
Herod, the child-slayer, who sacrificed righteous blood for the
        sake of a drink
and a daughter's lewd gyrations, or again the murderers of
        Christ
455 the King of all, and all the persecutors who arose
both before and after and during recent times,
of whom the first and last, Belial's evil chasm,
is the dire force of Julian, the destroyer of souls.   (557)
Smitten by God for raising up battle against Christ,

460 his dust is still hotly boiling, a great terror to evildoers.
    And those others whom marriage has given to life, and still will
        give,
    liars, murderers, the twisted, perjurers,
    stealers of others' things, violators of a stranger's bed—
    who could ever count them? For this is a thing that's plain for
        all to see,
465 that, as dust is more abundant than gold, so also the worst
        people are more numerous
    than the good: for, indeed, they travel upon unequal paths.
    For that of the evil is flat on the ground and makes for easy
        running.
    But the good make their way uphill. For this reason, as far as
        these excel in good,
    so far do the wicked excel in number.
470 If then you will leave off glorying in children
    and calling a maimed life the companion of divinity,   (558)
    we will end our argument right here. You can have the
        honor for which people contend.
    For I myself in no way begrudge this to an earthly parent.
    But if, having received from God second-rate things, you look
        for first-place honors,
475 I will pronounce my discourse truly, albeit grievous to the
        heart.
    Who among human beings ever contrived this thing, to sire
    the best of children? By what means is a deformed child
        produced?
    For a person draws, without degradation, an image from an
        image,
    and a modeler stamps out models that resemble their patterns,
480 and art hammers gold by hand, whatever way the mind directs,
    and a farmer reaps a good ear of corn from good grain,
    nor does his desire fail of its hoped-for purpose.

But a mortal knows not clearly the nature of his offspring, what
    sort of thing it'll be:
neither the bad know this, nor the good, though in fact the
    good pray better.
485 It might be that a man like Paul will produce a
    Christ-killing son,   (559)
an Annas, or a wicked Caiaphas, or some Judas;
or again, someone evil by nature, like Judas,
might be called the parent of most divine Paul, or of Peter
the unbreakable rock, and be the father of the one allotted the
    key.
490 Nor does a father know if he will produce a cherished
son or daughter. He has only quenched the flesh's raging in his
    bed.
From the one first parent came both Cain and Abel,
the one envious, the other the worthy farmer of the God-
    fearing sacrifice.
Isaac's children were both Esau the bad and excellent Jacob:
495 nay, more, the twin son of the identical parent differed.
And Solomon was wise at first; afterward, he was worst
when he had turned to sin, affected by womanish vices.
Or again, Paul's great power appeared in both respects:
first he dishonored Christ, but then he proclaimed him
    to all,   (560)
500 having turned his fiery force towards a good zeal.
Among these things, what shall we ascribe to marriage?
    Nothing, if you ask me.
For the image looked-for does not flow from a married couple.
But as someone who delights his mind in the turnings of dice
tosses them, but the odd or even come up, not by his hands,
505 but by the spontaneous turnings of the stones,
in the same way marriage, the sower of children, does not
    engender

intelligent or evil, but human nature or education teaches
   them.
But if you'd like to know a true saying: those who are best,
whether formed by spirit or by word, are best.
510 For the spark of godliness has been hidden in human
      beings,
   as in certain stones the power of fire. And as flame is produced
      from stones
   by the strikings of iron, so from mortal men
   instruction brings forth hidden godliness. But those
      who are worst   (561)
   pertain especially to marriage. For, indeed, it produces
      mostly here and now,
515 as a nail, in league with the changing world, binding the flesh
   earthwards, and a leaden weight burdening the soul
      downwards,
   and a similar allotment imitating one's parents here and now.
   All the same, let's make a deal concerning parents: if you don't
      mention
   those who are good, I'll stop harping on the evil ones.
520 But by other things, too, you might know how much better is
      the holy life,
   if you would examine both love for God and for the fat flesh,
   both the world's nature and its twofold ends.
   For if, in fact, you would dispel a bit the defiling rheum
   from your vision, or the mist from the morning light,
525 and would open your eyes to the light of our sun,
   and look on all things with a pure mind,   (562)
   then you would encounter Virginity entirely God's offering,
   brighter than gold or amber or ivory,
   sharp-seeing, calm, well-winged, head aloft,
530 cheerful, radiant, lifted above the ground, not stuck
   in earth's caverns, but inhabiting heaven's wide-founded

city, and dwelling far from the flesh,
taking hold with one of her hands unaging life,
with the other, unending wealth and glory:

535   not, indeed, the way a snail, burdened beneath its shell,
painfully drags its dripping body with sluggish steps;
nor, again, dividing herself between the Lord Christ and the
         flesh;
nor again, after the manner of amphibians, both claiming the
         dry land
and swimming night and morning in the sensuous
         waters;   (563)

540   but directing her whole intellect towards God, and from God
blooming with greater offspring than from parents,
blooming in hope, and in pure conceptions from him who is
         pure.
But Marriage, on the other hand, you would see running away
         from Christ
on account of the shakings of destroying dust and the
         multitudinous

545   cares of the world, or else only slightly adhering to God.
For as when someone beholds at the same time two heads or
         two faces,
or, again, sees written on a sheet of paper double letters,
she does not grasp the whole character exactly, even though
         she wants to,
but part of it she catches, part of it eludes her narrow, scattered

550   vision: so also a love that is parceled up,
part for the world and part for Christ, is feeble; but that which
         lasts is aimed at only one.
For either someone, holding on to Christ entire, gives no
         thought for a wife,
or else, honoring the love of dust, he has forgotten Christ.
At times before this I've seen a stonemason, or someone   (564)

555 skilled in working wood, men of prudence and know-how:
whenever they would mark off a line with a straightedge,
they close one of their eyes under its eyelids,
and, having directed all their gaze to the other eye, they are
    focused,
so that they attain precision, and the iron hits its mark.
560 In the same way, desire, when gathered into unity, drives
    nearest to Christ,
who desires the desirer, and beholds the beholder:
he beholds the beholder, and goes to meet the one
    approaching.
To the extent that anyone desires, and sees, to that same extent
    he has seen,
and so far he desires: the good circle is revolved in full.
565 Desiring this, then, I forsook this life, nor was capable
of casting my gaze elsewhere; for the sweet bond holds me
    back   (565)
when I am longing for that beauty that terrifies the mind
    of the one who looks upon it,
but on me it shakes out a fiery red brilliance
and sets me altogether beautiful and shining.
570 For only for one who loves does it gather from the beloved a
    share
of desires and beauty; and blessed is whoever has received of
    this.
But you, on the other hand, foster a different longing in your
    breast,
and, as though you were approaching thereby all the closer to
    heaven,
you take thought, you say, for children and property and
    parents,
575 as easy things, but, to her who is wise, a longing for what's easy
    is unprofitable:
a small boat, little means and slight profit

of unstable things. And this voyage of yours is infinite,   (566)
and, in traversing the straits, you pray for a successful passage,
spreading your sails out full as you cut through the Ionian
    waves.

580 The wind, if favorable, brings these things across and even
    what's better;
but, if it be contrary, dying out there is an insignificant fate.
Now, this is the great voyage of the soul and of the good spirit.
Trembling, then, at this, I have all the more laid hold on Christ;
and not only then, but even when the going is good, I long all
    the same

585 for my Christ, my holy love, who is steadfast to those who love
    him.
Again, whoever, in the midst of a craving, looks towards the
    hand of God,
appearing not to crave, swiftly loses the desire of the moment.
For if Christ would transfix your mind from above with
    his arrow   (567)
and would wound your midriff with his refreshing dart,

590 then, being initiated both ways into the mysteries of either
    kind of love,
you would know how much sweeter the Lord's good is.
What other arguments are there? Parents are rejuvenated in
    their sons,
who care for them in their old age; and both a husband finds
    youth in a wife, and a wife in her husband.
And joys and sorrows and worries held in common

595 are the lighter, and one who stands firm is a great support to
    one who limps.
But, in my view, all those are my parents who have taught me
    well,
and those are my children, whom I have taught. The sole
    spouse I've taken

is Christ, who embraces the unwedded above all others,
even if he was nailed for all, and raised up the cross for
    everyone's sake.
600 Jubilant in him even during bouts of depression   (568)
I rejoice, and he makes me buoyant even in grief,
like gold cleansed of dross in smelting furnaces.
But as ally of that temperance that, for you, marriage and the
    bond enforce,
I have placed, not the flesh, but the Word,
605 and the desire that, when strong, excludes what is weaker,
like some lion set over weaker animals.
For bodies become one of mind through sufferings;
for which reason they also know how to give some pleasure to
    each other.
For you, the table is laden, but a small crumb feeds me,
610 just as Christ also once fed the thousands in the
    wilderness.
For you there is drink each day, but my wine is always rich:
fountains and rivers and deep wells flow with it.
For you, sleek faces and glittering garments;   (569)
my ornament is dirty hair and poor clothing.
615 The garment I wear, shaking with golden tassels,
is Christ, the hidden, brilliant ornament of my soul.
For you the delectable bed, but my beddings are of
    sackcloth:
a rush mattress on the floor and the earth moistened with
    tears.
By you, gold is honored; by me, lovely dust.
620 You are giddier than a calf; my head is downcast in silence.
You burst out laughing; I never let loose my jaw.
You covet honor; my honor is not upon the earth.
But when you have considered and seen these things,
take a look also at the irksome aspects of marriage for those
    who adore the flesh.

625 A husband is sold to a wife, and, what's worse,
     often he is worthless; and a wife is sold to a husband,   (570)
     and is frequently despicable: a thoroughgoing evil,
           which can't be got rid of.
     For if, on the one hand, the people are good and agree with
           each other, when they come together
     the voyage of life is easier and mixed with a prosperous
           wind.
630 But if they are evil, behold! domestic suffering within, endless
           antipathy.
     But let us grant that they are not bad, and are in agreement.
           Still, frequently
     a heavy fate descends upon a newly-wedded couple.
     First a groom, then a corpse; the bedroom, then the tomb;
           anxieties
     unmixed with joys; a little melody before a symphony of
           sorrow.
635 One person lights the wedding torch; another quenches it.
     One child calls on his father's name; another man is
           suddenly
     childless, like a sapling shaken bare by the wind.   (571)
     Now a maiden, then a wife, then a widow.
     In one night, or often in a single day, all these things come to
           pass.
640 Tearing her braided hair, casting away her bridal
     regalia, rending her cheeks with imprecatory hands,
     having eschewed virginity's modesty for bitter passions'
           sake,
     she calls her husband ill-fated and bewails her empty home,
     her widow's bed, and her untimely grief.
645 I'll pass over in silence the misfortunes of childbearing, the
           dead burdens
     in the hollows of the womb, a bitter and motherless fruit,

not of children; rather, after being the children's tomb, then she
   gives birth:
corpses before their birthday, a childless childbearing.
I decline to mention, also, the untimely born, the braindead,
   and the disfigured,
650 a maiming of the human kind, and mockeries of the flesh. (572)
Were someone to weigh these things in the balance, he would
   see what way
the scale would drop, and how much my own life would
   ascend
towards the high-ruling God, plainly visible to all people of
   worth.
But I will be silent concerning others' shames: for thus it befits
655 Virginity's chaste mouth to avoid scurrilous talk.
Nevertheless, if you bring forth mocking accusations against
   deiform Virginity,
and if someone, perhaps, should denigrate somewhat my way
   of life,
and should mix Christ's unstained coat with shame,
having chosen, in his sins, your goods as primary,
660 being late-wed, and having fled the great life of holiness:
I, even I, will put you in mind of the most shameful bed of
   larceny,
that bed that the wicked steal, trampling underfoot God's
   warnings.
For this is the most destructive of all evils for mortals
and full of devouring fire consuming the inward parts,   (573)
665 when someone, full of base intent, approaches another man's
   bed
and leaves in doubt both the offspring and the bond of love.
But adulterers and reprobate fools don't keep you off
from marrying; and he weds, too, who thrusts into his enemy's
   flank

his adulterer-slaying sword, letting it still drop
670 with human gore, and dodging the rapier's sharp point.
      But who among such witless folk will separate me from
      the love of Christ? Or will a small pebble hold back a wide
              river?
      It is not right, it is not fitting; for it would be much better
      for some to fall while a majority are raised high (if it is
              legitimate to speak this way
675 in opposition to common speech), than that everyone
      should stay on the ground, in fear of some wing falling.
      For these are the excellent, Christ's glory, while the others are
              the worst:
      just as, when people sling a stone aloft into the sky,   (574)
      they receive a wound and shame upon their own
              witless heads.
680 Lucifer formerly was an angel. But, when he fell,
      his glory remained among the heavenly ones, just as Judas
      was no reproach to the disciples, when he fell, but he
              straightway
      was struck from the number of the elect, while the Eleven best
              disciples remained.
      And the sea has occasioned one man's destruction, but another
              sails on by, spreading wide
685 his white sails, observing the shipwreck's tomb; or else from
              that sepulcher
      he unties the cables for himself, and, on his own ship, he makes
              the stern-cables tight.
      O my Mother, do you still command me to leave the life that
              leads skywards,
      or should we end the discussion, since the victory belongs to
              your daughter?
      It's my victory, but a victory, too, for my parents. But if you are
              honored for having come to be
690 Virginity's mother, how much honor is mine?

Don't you perceive that all those whom you have cited   (575)
    as most excellent,
although from parents, were more just and better than their
    parents?
And Christ is from Mary; nevertheless, he is much better than
    she—
not only than Mary, and all those encompassed in the flesh,
695 but also than minds, as many as the far-flung heavens enfold.
And an ear of wheat comes from something tiny, but from its
    seed sprouts
the grain, and gold is greatly eminent over sand.
Here, then, is the completion of my discourse; may what I say
    reveal
an image, both for the virgin and the married life;
700 thus bear in mind my argument's conclusion.
There are flakes of snow, and springtime flowers,
the graying locks of the old and shriveled, and the strength of a
    stripling in his prime.
But it has happened ere now that flowers have been seen in
    winter, and wintry
snowflakes have sometimes been observed in days of
    spring.   (576)
705 And a youth has grown gray hairs, and I've seen a spry old man
much stronger than a lad at the first bloom of youth.
So, then, marriage, too, is earthly by nature, and unweddedness
is wedded to Christ the King of all. But, all the same,
every so often heavy virginity droops to the ground,
710 and marriage darts up heavenward, in which cases both,
unexpectedly, give a false impression, the one of Wedlock,
the other of Virginity.
But, O beloved parents and still-unmarried youths,
how long, after the pattern of creeping things or tortoises
or eight-footed crabs that walk athwart,

715 or like the twisted belly windings often-foot snakes,
     will you live burdened down by the hateful load of the flesh?
     Come then, and hearken to Christ's exhortation,
     and, casting aside beauty, fame, wealth, family, success, and all
          things   (577)
     (adamantine evil's pleasing productions)—
720 being roused from all that, let us go forth in the way of the life
          that is light,
     in total chastity, one in mind with the most pure beings of
          heaven,
     so that, standing in wait upon the great God,
     in joy we may sing to the Lord a festal hymn;
     and having left to marriage and irksome earth
725 the things that pursue the perishing, in exchange for the
          brilliance of paradise,
     let us return again to the glory of the unfettered life
     and to the goodly plant of the garden, from which I fell by my
          foolishness.
     So much, then, spoke godlike Independence. And the judges,
     although desiring Marriage, nevertheless will crown the head
730 of Virginity. But Christ, giving both of them a gift of   (578)
          honor,
     will set Virginity nearby at his right hand,
     and Marriage at his left, which thing, too, is a most high honor.

A Comparison of Lives

Poem 1.2.8, Comparatio vitarum (PG 37:649–667)

Lives) You be judge between us, stranger.
Judge) What's there to judge?
Lives) Two lives are at odds.
Judge) And who are they, and what's their dispute?
Lives) The worldly life and the life of the spirit:
which one is the better, and that which the wise would prefer
to live?
5 Judge) It's a hard matter to judge, but all the same worth
listening to.
Worldly Life [W]) Being born of the world, I know and love
the things of it,
and piety means respecting the code of one's fathers.
Spiritual Life [S]) Being born of God, I know and worship
God,
and piety means understanding perfect worship.
10 If with you what is inferior is most honorable,   (650)
why shouldn't I have more right, with what is better?
W) My mother is flesh, and I was mixed together with
dust;
I seek completion in that flesh from which I'm separated.
S) God is my father, and unto God I've been yoked;
15 I desire the imitation of that form from which I've
flowed.
W) Tell me, how would the human race exist

if not for our bodies being joined in marriage,
governed by divine law, and by nature likewise?
S) This is a law, yes, but one from which I now should be
    exempt,
20 since I strive after another life, greater than
this present one, free from bondage and corruption.
W) How has it come, then, this novel virgin lifestyle?
S) It existed even of old, in a shadowy way; but now it
    burns brightly,   (651)
ever since there appeared a virgin Mother of God.
25 And, in fact, the old law has made way for the new:
the letter has gone, the power of the spirit remains.
W) But what unmarried person would there *be,* if not for the
    married life,
or who'd be just? S) How adroit you are,
encouraging copulation, on account of the good;
30 but, while time has nourished both good people and bad,
the sower spews forth the hubris of the flesh.
Nothing else. To have one's mind set on passion,
as though this were cooperating with God's will,
    is ridiculous.
W) What then have you given to life? S) Why, what did you
    look for?
35 Branches? So that they should freeze, or get caught in a
    blizzard?
W) You give me my root, then you can keep your
    branches.   (652)
S) To be born is enough. Let someone else labor upon
    corruption,
feeding, teaching, then all of a sudden mourning
one who no longer exists, seeing engraved on the wall
40 his lifeless beauty, a son who lies still.

W) Well, I at least am from a noble family.
S) What kind of family?
And what kind of maker? Do you not realize
that you are clay? One thing is well-bred, to imitate God.
You're strong in tombs and new declarations:
45 from this you're styled as noble, but you haven't lived so.
W) For me, money-making overthrows enemies,
it consumes bad men with envy, it wins friends;
it hands out thrones, making you look big in the city.
S) For me, being poor gives the gift
50 of having no enemies, and pity's a safer investment   (653)
    than envy.
Thrones are perishable, and friends may last but awhile.
And even if these do remain, it's better to give God
    first place,
and either possess the principles of all things visible,
or else be high above all visible things.
55 Then the noetic city might hold me resplendent.
W) But what security is there in an impoverished life?
Walls and gates, tricksters, men with switchblades.
S) Why should we struggle, if we have only the body
    to steal?
It has only itself and a little rag.
60 Let the thief be for others, let the tyrant be gone!
The burglar attacks proprietors; as for me, God is my sole
    wealth:
once one has acquired him, no one can ever steal
    him away.
But as for those other things, dear to those who have
    them, let
any hand snatch this substance away from me.   (654)
65 Nothing is more secure than a poor man:
the rich man sacrifices to his net; the pledge that he gives

is for his own self, he greets it as a friend;
and he does not hymn God, the giver of all good things
until his acquisitions fall into a stranger's hands
70 in spite of himself—what am I saying? perhaps they go to his
        enemies,
and thence to someone else, with the turnings of a wheel of
        torment.
But, when I die, life will have been all to my profit,
leaving nothing to spite and turns of fate.
W) How much better not to have to look for help from
        neighbors,
75 but that others, even those more religious, should look
        to us?
S) How much better to look for help to God alone,
who, like a father, gives when he is asked,
and not to accept something shameful, on account of   (655)
        one's business,
in imitation of a blood-sucking leech,
80 latching upon these things, aiming one's wits at those,
        peering at this with eyes up to no good,
picturing that in the wishes of one's dreams,
being ever the poorer, on account of the desired object.
W) How then shall someone bear the brunt of bitter times,
85 having nothing to shore him up in his misfortune?
S) Are you asking me how to dodge a well-aimed arrow?
A hair is hard to split, even from up close.
Grow slim for me, and you'll slip past the force of the
        wicked.
A reed can withstand the winds, while trees cannot,
90 for, where this gives way, the winds' weight knocks
        those over.
W) I can live in luxury. S) My luxury
is to have no luxury, with its bloatedness, its intestinal

swellings, its sickening with wealth's dyspepsia,   (656)
a smelling of treacly sludge outside the throat,
95 the mind diminishing as the mud grows thicker.
W) I eat cake. S) Bread's my pudding,
apples are my food, and all my sweets are briny.
I spit out the sour food of hedonists.
W) Well, I at least am pleased with perfumes' scents,
100 with songs, the clappings of hands and feet, well-timed
        breakings,
a symphony of instruments in concert.
S) Such are the things you commend, but such are the
        things,
I think, that an evil rich man goes for, as a teacher of evils.
For us, there's a better psalmody than from instruments:
105 the soul that harmonizes with the noumena;
and Christ is sweeter smelling than any myrrh,
who for us became empty, to destroy the horrid stench
with which I was filled, from the gangrene of sin.   (657)
And I'll clap hands if my assassin falls,
110 who would lead me towards some evil word
or deed. Our dancing of feet? A strophe inspired by God.
W) Maybe you'll claim that poverty prevents diseases, too,
bringing bodies added remedies.
S) That I would not say, for it's not a true assertion.
115 But what is true, I'll state.
Those who live in poverty are a good deal healthier.
And God has granted each a commensurate favor:
to the poor, strength, to those with money, medicines.
The poor man toils, and evacuates fluids through sweat:
120 in hunger, in cold, scorched by the midday sun
he journeys, bears burdens, gets drenched, groans.
The food he finds is what's in season, simple and
        unadorned: (658)

he knows no fancy concoctions
that cooks and caterers of luxury
125 put together from the far corners of the earth and sea,
decking out an effeminate table for men.
Gases, catarrhs, disorders of the spleen, dislocated
        joints,
cries, excess fat, sallow complexions, the enfeeblings of
the well-to-do: all these are the products of excess.
130 They don't even possess the things that give them
        pleasure,
and they seek poundage in things they should avoid,
often becoming weaker when they strive for fitness:
destitute of everything, unfortunate in their success.
Gold, stones, embroidered robes, painters'
135 daubings and purple against the skin,
mosaics on the walls, on ceilings, and underfoot,   (659)
silver, too (some hidden away in cellars underground,
from which it's brought, appropriate for tombs;
some used for ornament, glimmering round
        drinking-cups),
140 horses, carpets, chariots, charioteers,
hounds, huntsmen, trackers of beasts;
and again, a wicked lady has such items for her pleasure,
on behalf of her stomach, and the sluice of an all-accepting
        gullet:
bed-dressers, porters, heralds, attendants at sleep,
145 flower-bearers, perfume-scatterers, hairdressers,
tasters, shade-bearers, butlers on the double,
bath-girls and wine-pourers at the lifting of a finger,
lissome women, the eyes' delectation:
all this for an opulent tomb, an inscription of dust!
150 But the poor man stands, and even if he falls,   (660)
struggling with sickness, hardly ever is it for long;

he will show nothing of it to his friends,
but will die like a lion, still roaring at his end,
much more cheerful, all told, than the affluent.
155 What else? Audacity, a temper, raving, boasting,
drunkenness, unchecked laughter, shameful talk,
superciliousness to God, to kindred and to friends:
these things pertain, not to the poor, but rather the rich.
For wealth brings pride, which brings, again, destruction.
160 Whereas, in most cases, a man weighed down is not lifted up,
but the fear of God accrues to him especially, a companion,
a potent guide to everything that's good.
Briefly consider these lives, one against one,
and towards them both remain an honest judge: (661)
165 don't you even take this for a show of arrogance,
when the poor gather round nearby you,
or breathe the same air as you, or are called by
one same name, so as to seem your familiars or
    shipmates?
You resent the good, I pity the evil.
170 For nothing is more miserable than the wicked,
even if they race successfully towards a slippery goal.
You spit at the poor, as if he were from another God;
I know one creation, with all of us coming to
a single judgment. But the new creation brings morality.
175 Things fortunate work you up; I am prudent, in fear.
Your setbacks depress you; I am light with my hopes.
For nothing stays constant, but flows away in length
    of time.
Night's given rest to day, and day to night;
and sorrow's put a stop to joy, and enjoyments   (662)
180 to profit: don't hold on, then, to these things, as though they
    were permanent.
To you, nothing is ominous, even if grossly evil.

Your luxury somehow gets in the way of your senses.
But I am sorrowful even over minor things.
For sin is an estrangement from God.
185 How should I bear God, in a state of loss?
For you, sleep is satisfying, and you lay down on both
        sides.
Sweet are the dreams that mirror the day's events.
You drink, you dice, you clutch, you flirt, you laugh.
For me, the greater part of life is sleepless.
190 For pains stab at me even when I lie resting,
and when I do snatch a little sleep, I weep.
And the rude night's appearances frighten me,
the judgment, a judge not well-disposed to me,
        while I stand there trembling;
here a fountain with fire unquenchable boiling;   (663)
195 there, a worm forever gnawing;
in the middle, conscience, an unwritten prosecutor.
God will be your God if he gives you the things you like;
for me, he's to be honored, even if he gives the contrary.
For his wearying of me is a medicine of salvation.
200 To the extent that I'm weighed down, to that extent
I come close to God: for suffering binds me tight to God.
For even an approaching army drives a people inside their
        walls.
Children, a wife, and friends are your comforters—
but a great misfortune alters these.
205 But God is my support and consolation,
when I am hungry, shivering, and in straits.
Go on, act tough, beat up on me, call me low-born
        and poor,
stomp and push; you won't be acting tough much longer.
By God I endure all things, and it's to him I look.   (664)
210 I direct my thoughts to the life hereafter;

that's where I dwell, I know nothing of things here below.
By such means I am easily delivered from sorrow.
Something else? No, you won't get the vote
today, it seems to me, nor can you stomach this.

215 For he who always masters cannot stand to be mastered.
To me it's all the same, whether I win or lose.
God is enough for me, even if another bears off all the rest.
This is victory's greatest prize of glory, by my thinking.
W) What then if some should fall from the highest things?

220 S) What then if some should fall from things in
          second place?
For, in truth, standing straight and falling apply to both.
All things being equal, I myself count it much worse
for them that fall while in the premier life;
so much am I opposed to anything evil.   (665)

225 For, the more honorable the strength of those who
          triumph,
the more miserable is their fall, when they trip up.
But this I ask of you, not to consider whether someone is
worst in his way of life; for he is contrary to his own life.
But inspect and evaluate, in the same person's case,

230 the mode of things both good and evil, comparing them,
and do not discard what's worst when attached to something
          else,
since this is unfair, and undercuts most everything.
But, to determine these lives' ratio,
do not set me the best of asses against an evil horse,

235 nor again the finest man of a worldly life
against the worst one of our company.
For, that the former would appear superior, I won't deny.
But if you place highest next to highest, side by side, and
worst by worst, you'll learn to what extent I'm stronger.   (666)

240 And observe this too: how far falling always
pertains to you, and overcoming to us.

     For, as they say, one swallow does not a good spring make,
     nor one white hair old age.
     What do you say? Do you give your vote? Can I celebrate?
245 Judge) I give it. How couldn't I? I suppose I'd have to
     prefer the lower life to yours
     when, out of my mind, I should count some mortal man God's
         equal.
     But if I am not out of my mind, this is a thing I shall not think.
     But hold off; the best thing is for both of you
250 to behave yourselves peaceably, both towards each other and
         before the mighty God,
     with you distributing your first-fruits to the first-place life,
     and you, again, receiving the second-place life as brother.
     If in fact he doesn't have what's first, what should
         prevent him   (667)
     from having what's second? There's no dishonor in this.
255 In this way, our life may be preserved from danger.

Conversation with the World

Poem 1.2.11, Dialogus cum mundo (PG 37:752–753)

Quest.) I've an issue, world, to bring up with you. Who are
    you, and
whence, teach first, and whither do you roll?
And how do you revolve me, like a wheel that carries an ant?
Ans.) Where I'm from I don't know, but I know it's from God.

5 And I roll towards something greater. But I don't turn   (753)
    you round.
But it's you, unworldly one, who act violently towards me.
Quest.) How then do you stand solid, whilst I'm unsteady?
Ans.) I am something external, and what's the advantage of
    that?
But the things you want to do, you can do them, if you want.

10 Quest.) Well and good; but external things, who can bear
    them?
Ans.) Why, is there something wrong?
Matter here is for the sake of the salvation of the good.
Quest.) Then, the cause of you is someone greater? Ans.)
    You've got it.

On the Precariousness of
Human Nature

Poem 1.2.12, De naturae humanae fragilitate (PG 37:754)

Dear world, though not so very dear, why like a rolling wheel
do you bear down on me, who trudge wheezing
like a tiny ant distressed at his sore burden?   (754)
But you who are so huge, on the other hand, bear so much.
5   I know, in fact, that you are from God, proclaiming him.
        But likewise, formed
by Christ's own hand, you were woven of things
both heavenly and earthly. The body was fashioned down here,
while soul, again, is a breath of the great Mind.
Nevertheless, like all the others, I am driven to and fro
10   by my miseries, miseries from an enemy.
And like a seagoing dolphin upon land, in the thin air I die.
World, my time is done; bring the people on unwounded.

On the Precariousness of
Human Nature

Poem 1.2.13, De naturae humanae fragilitate (PG 37:754-755)

Myself and time, like birds
or ships at sea, slip past each other,
with nothing that stays put;   (755)
but what I've done amiss does not skip by,
but stays: this is life's cruelest pain.
5   Nor can I tell what to pray for, to live on, or be done:
it's fearful either way. Come, think with me.
Through sins my life's become an aching mess. But if I die,
ai ai! there's no cure then for your old passions!
If this is what life appoints for you, its anguish is so great
10   that even when ended it holds no end of troubles,
but on both sides there's a precipice. What's there to say? This
      then is what's best,
to look towards you alone, and your kindheartedness.

On Human Nature

Poem 1.2.14, De humana natura (PG 37:755–765)

Yesterday, worn out with anxieties, away from others
I was in a shady grove, my soul consumed.
For how I do so love this drug for sufferings,   (756)
to speak in quiet, me with my own soul.
5   And the breezes whispered while the birds sang,
granting from the branches a sound slumber,
though for a soul quite weary. While, from the trees,
deep chanting, clear-toned, lovers of the sun,
whirring locusts made the whole wood to resound.
10 Nearby flowed cold water by one's feet,
gently coursing through the cool grove. But as for me,
the strong sorrow I had had, I had it still.
Therefore, I didn't care about these things, since a mind
cloaked round with sorrows doesn't want to sing back
      happily.
15 But privately, my mind in a whirlpool spinning,
I had this sort of battling round of words:
Who was I? Who am I? What shall I be? I don't know
      clearly.   (757)
Nor can I find one better stocked with wisdom.
But, as through thick fog, I wander
20 every which way, with nothing, not a dream, of the things I
      long for.
For all of us are groundlings, vagabonds, over whom
the swart cloud of the fat flesh hangs.

But wiser than me is he who, beyond others,
expelled from his heart its ready-spoken lie.
25 I am. Think: what does this mean? Something of me's
    gone by,
something I'm now completing, another thing I'll be, if I will
    be.
Nothing's for sure. I am, indeed, a troubled river's current,
always in transit, having nothing fixed.
Which of these, then, will you say that I am?
And what I am more than yourself, come teach me.
30 Now, stick with this, and watch, or I'll escape you.   (758)
You won't go twice through that same flow of river
that you traversed before, neither will you see the same man
as he is at present. Present I was in my father's flesh;
my mother then received me, and I was of them both. After
    this
35 a glob of flesh, unhuman, too hideous for beholding,
    of neither
reason nor mind partaking, having my mother for a tomb.
We're buried twice, we live upon decay. For this life's road I go,
I see it as the years' expense
that ravaging old age has dished me out. And if thence
40 eternity receives me, with no wasting, as is said,
consider whether life holds not its death, whereas the end
may yet be life for you, contrary to what you think.
I'm a nothing. Why am I so pommeled down by ills,   (759)
    like a thing compacted?
For, for those whose time is brief, this only is constant,
45 innate, unshakable, unaging. When I had slipped
out of my mother's womb, I first let go a tear; though,
for all the kinds of grief I was to meet,
I should have tried to weep before this life.
Now, we've heard of places free of wild beasts, as Crete was
    once,

50   and places strangers to cold wind-borne clouds;
     but no one among mortals has ever made this boast, that,
     unvanquished, he has left life's hateful pains.
     Feebleness, poverty, birth, death, enmity, rogues,
     sea-beasts and land-beasts, sufferings: all this is life.
55   I have known many woes and utter unhappiness,
     but of good things, nothing wholly free from pain,   (760)
     from the time that that bitter price got wiped on me
     by the destroying taste, and the adversary's spite.
     Well, so much, flesh, for you, incurable, an agreeable
60   enemy, who never lets up warring,
     a beast sharply biting, a fire that chills, what a wonder!
     It'll be a great wonder, if ever you end up agreeable to me.
     To you, soul, shall things hereon be said, as many as is
          fitting.
     Who, what, whence are you? Or who set you about
65   carrying a corpse, and locked you in the hateful chains
          of life,
     always loaded down to earth? How have you mingled
     spirit and fat, the flesh with the mind, what is weightless
          with a burden?
     For these things fight in mutual opposition.
     If then you entered life co-planted with the flesh: (761)
70   Ah, how, from afar, has this yoke of marriage shattered me!
     I am an image of God, and have turned out a son of shame;
     I blush at honor's mother, craving lust.
     For a liquid engendered me, and it dried up: now a man,
          then again
     no man, but dust: these are your last hopes.
75   But if heavenly, who, and whence are you? Teach him who
          longs to know.
     If a breath and particle of God, as you conceive,
     cast out depravity, and I' ll believe. For it's no way right

for slime to abide in what's clean, no, not a bit.
For there is no dark particle from the sun, neither has there
80 shone from a wicked spirit a radiant offspring.
Or how do you get propelled by deadly Belial's
          incitements,
soul, if indeed with heavenly Spirit you've been blended? (762)
For if, with such a helper, you still tilt towards the earth,
ai ai your noxious evil must be undiluted!
85 But if you didn't come to me from God, what then is your
          nature?
In fact, there's a great fear that I might be puffed up with a vain
          boast.
Formation by God, paradise, Eden, fame, hope, a
          commandment,
a world-destroying rainstorm, a storm of a fiery
          firmament;
then the law, a written remedy; and after that
90 Christ, blending his own form with ours, so that
God, by his passion, might give me a defense against my
          passions,
and perfect me as god by his human image.
Nevertheless, I keep an unchanging bent, while we rush
upon the sword in suicidal madness, like the swine.
95 What's in fact the good of life? God's light? But then   (763)
hateful and jealous darkness keeps me from it.
Nothing's of any use to me. And what is there of no use to the
          wicked?
If only they were equally endowed, with troubles especially!
I lie helpless. Divine terror has bowed me.
100 I'm worn out by worries, night and day.
This thick-necked one has knocked sleep, too, behind me,
and stomped it under foot. But tell me, you, your slue of
          horrors:

     dismal Tartarus, flame-scorchers, quirts,
     demons, the debt-collectors of our souls.
105 To the wicked, all a myth: they just value the here
        and now;
     torture doesn't turn round wickedness.   (764)
     Better that transgressors in the end be left unpunished
     than that the sufferings of vice should now depress me.
     But why me? Why's it for me to sing so much of humankind's
        misfortunes?
110 The ache exists for each one of our race.
     It's not by me that the earth goes unshaken, the gales batter the
        seas;
     and the hours give way to each other in a rush:
     night's laid rest to day, the air's grown thick with cold.
     The stars by the sun, and the sun by a cloud
115 find their beauty expunged: and the moon revives.
     Again, this heaven, full of stars, is half as bright.
     And you, Lucifer, were once among the angelic choirs,
     O evil-eyed! but you've dropped now shamefaced from the
        heavens.
     Be merciful to me, O Trinity, cherished kingdom:
     not even you   (765)
120 entirely escaped the tongue of senseless mortals.
     First the Father, afterward the great Child, and then the great
        God's
     Spirit is attacked by scurrilous words.
     Where will you stop while carrying me further, bad-counseling
        worry?
     Stop. Everything is secondary to God. Give in to reason.
125 God didn't make me in vain. I am turning
     my back upon this song: this thing was from our
        feeblemindedness.

Now's a fog, but afterward the Word, and you'll know all,
whether seeing God, or eaten up by fire.
Now, when the beloved mind had sung for me these things,
130 it digested its pain. And late from the shady grove I headed
     home,
now laughing at this self-estrangement, then once again
heart in anguish smoldering, from a mind at war.

On the Cheapness of the Outward Man

Poem 1.2.15, De exterioris hominis vilitate
(PG 37:766–778)

Who was I? Who am I? What will I become before long?   (766)
And where will you bring your great creature to rest,
>   Immortal One,
if, as I wonder, there is anything great in beings who are
>   nothing,
we mortal men, who uselessly stretch the brow.
5   If what we are were this alone, which has been shown to all,
and life's destroyed, I should have nothing more.
A young calf abandons the entrails of his dam,
he frolics, and nudges the sweet udder.
And at three he takes up the yoke, and hauls a wagon's
>   payload,
10   adding his mighty neck to the neck of the strong.
And a shimmery-skinned fawn, having slipped out from the
>   womb,
straightway sets feet to feet alongside her mother,
and can flee both flesh-devouring dogs, and the swift   (767)
>   horse,
and lie hidden with rabbits in thick bramble.
15   But bears, and the ravaging boars' breed, and lions,
the hurricane-like tiger, and the leopard's power,

when they glimpse iron, straightway their hair stands
    on end:
it stands on end, and they spring upon the sturdy huntsmen.
Again, a bird first lacks wings, but she's fair-winged
    before long,
20 and roams the air way up above the housetops.
Furthermore, the tawny bee forsakes his hole, and builds a
    house
instead, filling the residence with his sweet produce.
And all this is the work of one spring, when spontaneous
grows food for all, as the earth supplies a feast.
25 No vessels cleave the sea for them, nor do they plow;
they have no housemaids, or bearers of cups.
The swift wing feeds the bird, and the vale the beast,   (768)
who are made to work little, whose care is but of a day.
The great lion, too, as he licks the beast he's killed
30 (so I have heard), disdains to eat the remnants of his meal.
Sometimes he feasts daily, sometimes again
he laps drink, bravely bearing his belly its portion.
Life for these is so much the freer from toil:
home is always at hand among the rocks and branches,
35 cozy, sturdy, very beautiful. And if sickness
subdues them, ungrieving they abandon their stout breath.
They do not stand around keening in lamentable songs
one to another, nor do friends shave off their locks.
I'll say yet more: they meet their end here calmly,
40 the beast does not tremble at evil when he dies.
Now observe also the wretched race of men, as you
    might call it: (769)
in truth, there's nothing feebler than us humans.
From a fluid I'm produced, and in pangs my mother
    bore me;
I was raised thanks to many a hateful toil.

45 In her arms my mother bore me, a sweet travail; whereupon
    out on the ground I went, bruised and aching.
    Then I moved four-legged upon the earth. Next, I picked up
    my wobbling steps, held up by hands.
    Next, the mind started glowing, in a speechless voice's traces.
50 After this, I wept under literary tutelage.
    At twenty I gathered up strength, and went out to encounter
    many struggles, like a triumphant athlete.
    Other things I've had: some have vanished, some you've
        toiled at,
    as well you've known, my soul, in traversing this life:
55 an unbelievable undertow, a savage current,
        a heaving of the sea,   (770)
    here and there hurled up by the pounding winds.
    Much have I been shaken by stupidities; and much has the
        demon
    adversary of our life brought on besides.
    For if you should counterpose all life's pleasures and pains,
60 drawing up the balance in the midst,
    the scale weighed full with evil would sink down to
        the earth,
    while the side with good would shoot back up again.
    Combat, the sea, the field, labor, pilferers,
    acquisition, tax assessors, tax collectors, loudmouths,
65 orators, books, judges, a sacrilegious ruler:
    all these are this dismal life's enjoyments.
    Consider, again, these pleasures: bloatedness, loadedness,
        singing, and laughter,
    the tomb forever filled with clammy corpses,
    wedding gifts, marriage, another when the first breaks up, (771)
70 adulterers, their killers, children who cause suspicion's
        anguish,
    beauty, a faithless allure, ugliness, a fearless evil,

the worries of the high-born, the low-born's miseries,
wealth and poverty's twofold evil, arrogance, sickness:
a ball of novelties has bounced back into our hands.
75   In view, therefore, of these things, I am eaten up within,
       wondering whether anyone can suppose
that this is best, where what's bad outweighs what's good.
Don't you weep when you hear how much suffering was also
       of old?
I cannot tell if you'll weep or laugh in hearing it.
For the wise, again, both things would coincide:
80   some found cause of tears, others of laughter: (772)
as when Trojans and Achaeans smashed heads,
slaughtering one another, on account of a petty whore.
The Curetes, too, and the Aetolians staunch in battle, fought
over a swine's head, and a piglet's bristles.
85   Aiakos' kin were hymned at large, but they died, the one by
       enemies'
furious hands, the other by pure lechery.
Amphitryon's son Hercules had a great fame, but he, the all-
destroyer, succumbed to a flesh-consuming garment.
Neither Cyrus nor Croesus evaded a bad end,
90   nor did so many of our erstwhile emperors.
And you, dragon-like force unstoppable, wine did you in, (773)
Alexander, when you had overrun all the earth.
What good are the decomposed? They are but dust and
       bones,
the hero Agamemnon, Iros the vegetarian.
95   The emperor Constantine, and my page: one was unlucky,
the other, super-rich; now, only their tombs differ.
So goes it here; but concerning another existence,
       who's to say?
What things shall the unrighteous receive on that last day:

fire that roars, a gruesome darkness, to be far away
    from light,
100 the worm, the ceaseless remembrance of our own evil.
Better had it been for you, vile man, if you'd never crossed life's
    gates—
or if, having crossed them, like the beasts you'd perished
    utterly,
rather than to find again, after all your sufferings here,
yet worse punishments than those you've already met.
105 Where is my forefather's great honor? It perished with
    his meal.
Where's sharp-witted Solomon? Conquered by his wives. (774)
Where is he who was counted among the twelve, Judas,
who, for a little gain, was flooded round with darkness?
O Lord Christ, I beg you, grant right soon a cure for evils,
110 causing your servant to arise from out of here,
    O Blessed One!
For humans, there's but one thing safe and sound:
heavenly hopes, of which I breathe but little.
Of other goods I've had an abundant glut. Such things as
schlep along the ground, I long to leave them all to mortal
    men:
115 homeland, foreign lands, sees, and the prayer to be done with
    one's see,
neighbors, strangers, the pious, the wicked,
the forthright, the secretive, those whose eye bears no malice,
those who pine with suicidal evil within.
Leave life's pleasures to others: I shall most eagerly avoid
    them.
120 Ho the sufferings of this most lengthy life!
How long to keep producing turds? Just so, everything
    valuable   (775)
in this life of ours has a two-edged benefit:

it is both received and discarded by measure, day by day.
The throat holds some, the sewer all the rest.
125 Winter again, summer again, springtime, fall, in alternation;
days and nights, the dual perspective of our lives;
heaven, the earth, the sea: there's nothing in this that's new to
    me,
neither in what stands still, nor what keeps turning.
Enough with them! Give me, please, another life, another
    world:
130 striving for this, I'll bear all sufferings gladly.
If only I had died when wrapped up in my mother's womb,
and when the tears first came, there had been darkness!
What is life? I've leapt from one tomb, I go to another,
and after that tomb, I'll be buried in fire, uncared for.   (776)
135 This little I breathe is a swift-running river's flow,
always receding and returning again,
having nothing stable: it's only dust that flies into
my eyes, so that I tumble far below God's lights,
feeling my way about the walls, and wandering here
    and there.
140 Let me keep my two feet out of this great life.
I'll venture to make this true assertion: that man therefore
is God's toy, like one of the ones they feature in the cities.
On top is an extra, handmade face; if this gets lifted off,
I am ashamed, and suddenly I'm shown to be somebody
    else.
145 Such is the entire life of miserable men, whose
        preoccupations
are like the hopes of dreams. These things you have
        but briefly.
But I who have clung to Christ will never let go,   (777)
even when loosed from this earthly life's chains.
For, in truth, I am twofold: the body was formed down here,

150 and, again, it therefore nods down towards this ground.
But the soul is a breath of God, and always yearns exceedingly
for a greater share of the things of heaven above.
Like a fountain's flow is its trajectory; bounding upwards,
it knows the brilliant path of fire as the one thing changeless.
155 So great is man, as a very angel; when he jumps away,
like a serpent, old and spotted, off he goes.
Yes leap, ye priests, I'm dead. And you, wicked neighbors,
don't be frightened of me as formerly.
Fortify for yourselves the eternal Lord's   (778)
160 great house. But I, having left off all, retain one thing:
the cross of my life, a shining pillar. And so, when I arise
from hence, and am joined to celestial burnt offerings,
there will be no envy, a created evil, if it's right to call it this,
when, unenvying, I will pray for the envious, too.

On the Different Walks of Life

Poem 1.2.16, De vitae itineribus (PG 37:778–781)

Who, and whence, was I upon entering life? And after the
    earth receives me,
who shall I be when again I arise from the dust?
And where shall the great God place me, when he takes me?
    Will he save me, then,
raising me out from here into a clear harbor?
5   Many pathways are there to this much-enduring life,   (779)
with different troubles incident to each.
And in human matters, no good exists without its mix of evil.
If only miseries hadn't so great a part!
Wealth is unreliable, royalty a dreamy boast,
10   labor has its taskmaster, and poverty has chains.
Beauty's glamor's a little gift: youth's but
for a spell; white hair, a painful close to one's career.
Winged words? fame is a vapor; old blood
has breeding, true, but so does a wild boar.
15   A violent man's hard to bear; marriage is a bond; good
children are a cause of worry; bad ones, a malaise.
Markets are schools of vice; solitude brings
debilitude; the workplace, merely earthbound thoughts.
Stale is another's flatbread. Tilling the soil's
20   a chore. Of sailors, most wind up in the deep.   (780)
At home, one's in a cave; abroad, in disgrace.
Everything here is trouble for us mortals. All's laughter,

powder, shadows, illusions, dew, a breath, a wing, a puff, a
    dream,
a wave's heave, a river's flow, a schooner's trail, a breeze, fine
    dust,
25   a still-rolling circle, turning all alike,
the slow, the swift, the failures, the successful,
for hours, days, nights, with pains, deaths, sufferings
and pleasures, in illnesses, mishaps, triumphs.
And this, Creator Word, is of your wisdom, that instability
30   should be in everything, so we might have a love for what is
    stable.
I've surveyed everything on wings of mind, both things
    ancient
and new; and nothing is as feeble as us humans.
There's one thing good and safe for human beings: (781)
to leave here bearing a cross:
35   with tears, groans, the mind intent on things divine,
hope, and a light from the heavenly Trinity
mingling with the pure; a release from senseless dust;
the incorruption of the image received from God;
and to live another life's existence, exchanging
40   world for world, and bearing every burden.

Blessings of Various Lives

Poem 1.2.17, Variorum vitae generum beatitudines
(PG 37:781–786)

Blessed is he, whoever leads a solitary life, not at all mixing
with worldly folk, but has divinized the mind.
Blessed is he who, dwelling amidst many people, does not
    turn towards
the many, but directs his whole heart to God.   (782)
5   Blessed is he who purchases Christ with all his belongings
and has, as his only possession, the cross, which he raises on
    high.
Blessed is he who, administering his cleanly-gained
    possessions,
extends God's hand to those who are in need.
Blessed is the life of the joyous celibates, who are close
10 to the pure Godhead, having shaken off the flesh.
Blessed is he who, having yielded a little to the bonds of
    marriage,
bears the greater share of his love to Christ.
Blessed is he who, having authority over the people, by
holy and great sacrifices brings Christ to earthly folk.
15 Blessed is the one, who, being a child of the flock,
a most perfect nursling, keeps the place of the heavenly
    Christ.
Blessed is he who, by his pure mind's forceful movements, (783)
beholds the brilliance of the heavenly lights.

Blessed is he who honors the Lord by much-toiling hands: and,
20 for many people, this is the law of life.
All these things fill up the heavenly receptacles
in which are stored the fruit of our souls,
whilst every several virtue leads to a different place.
For many are the mansions pertaining to different lives.
25 Blessed is he, whom the mighty Spirit has shown to be poor in
        passions,
whoever leads a life of repentance;
who can never get his fill of celestial food;
who, by kindness, becomes inheritor of great things;
who, by bowels of mercy, draws down God's great
        compassion,
30 being a friend of peace and pure in heart;
who, for the sake of the great-famed Christ, has endured
        many   (784)
sufferings, and will find great honor.
Keep to the way of these people, whichever you prefer. If all of
        them,
that is best; if a few, a second good; if only one in particular,
35 even that is beloved. There are stations meet for everyone,
some for the more perfect, others for the lesser.
Rahab also led an indecorous life, but then her most sublime
hospitality made even her renowned.
And the publican had but one advantage over the Pharisee:
40 his lowliness of mind, as opposed to the other's self-exaltation.
Better it is to be unmarried, yes, better; but even that can be
        embroiled
in worldliness; and earthly-minded virginity is inferior to a
        sober
couple. Lofty is the life of those without possessions, who dwell
        upon the mountains;
but often vanity places even them below.

45 For they cannot compare their own virtue with others (785)
    who are excellent,
when pride stands unexamined in their heart.
And often those with fervent minds, like most hot-blooded
    colts,
bear their feet far wide of the turning post.
For which reason, either completely raise yourself upon light
    wings
50 or else keep below and run securely,
lest by being overburdened your wing should droop towards
    the ground,
lest, having been raised up, you should fall a most miserable
    fall.
A small ship fitted together with close-set bolts
bears a heavier freight than a large ship, poorly constructed.
55 Strait is the way of the divine gate,
but there are many paths that lead into that one.
Some take one route, as many as nature has inclined that way,
others take another, clinging to the strait path alone.
There is not one common food that pleases all alike, (786)
60 neither is there but one way of life appropriate to Christians.
For everyone, tears are best, and vigils and labors,
to hold in check the raging of grievous passions,
to conquer excess, to lie under Christ's strong hand,
and to tremble at the prospect of the approaching day.
65 And if you travel perfectly this high road, no longer are you
    mortal,
but one of the heavenly host. These are the laws of Gregory.

Concerning Human Life

Poem 1.2.18, De vita humana (PG 37:786–787)

From dirt to mud, then back to dust again.
For earth is reunited again with earth,
and in earthly swaddling-clothes is swaddled,
and dirt once more flies forward like the dust
5   that the violent twisting of the winds   (787)
lifts up on high, then throws back down.
And so it is with our much-swirling life
that the heady winds of wickedness
raise up on high, to spurious acclaim.
10 But again the dirt drops down, and stays below,
until the Creator's Word accords
the things conjoined their necessary parting.
But now there peers out, as if from some depth,
the dirt, made spiritual by the divine image,
15 and cries aloud in earthly tragedies,
and weeps this life, which seems to be a joke.

To His Former Congregation, Anastasia

Poem 2.1.6, Ad plebem Anastasiae (PG 37:1023–1024)

The ways of Zion mourn; the law's servant
longs for the people upon the feast days.
And I mourn for the people I don't see,
racing to hear my words, as did once
5   the people of Constantinople, and the strangers
therein dwelling, so many as the blessed Trinity had
      touched.
But now I, like a bellowing lion,
groan at length. And perhaps now others   (1024)
make off with my children, stealing them
10 through persuasive speech. For if strength would come to me
as before, O Trinity, then would I bellow again
in you, and perhaps the beasts would withdraw again a little.

Against a Demon

Poem 2.1.21, In diabolum (PG 37:1280)

Deliver, deliver me, Incorruptible One,
from an alien hand:
lest I should labor in evil works,
and Pharaoh should afflict me,
5   lest your enemy should keep me down
in bondage, O Christ,
and draw me into stony Babylon
beset by curses.
But let me remain in your temple,
10 stalwart, a songwriter.
Let no fiery shower of Sodom
drop down from above me.
But by the overshadowing of your mighty hand
drive far from me all sufferings.

On His Own Verses

Poem 2.1.39, In suos versus (PG 37:1329–1336)

Seeing many writing in this present life
words without measure, smoothly rolling,
who pass most time in drudgeries
producing only a hollow logorrhea,
5 and how they write so brazenly
things clogged full of idiocies,
as sand fills the sea or fruit-flies Egypt: (1330)
I've found this to be
the single sweetest counsel, that,
pitching out all other word, one hold
10 on only to those inspired by God,
as a calm harbor for those who flee the storm.
For if the Scriptures provide such a handle
—the Spirit—it's for you the wisest course
that you should be a citadel
15 from all vain words, for those who've started poorly.
Why, friend, not write words
free of doubt, in place of nether-stretching thoughts?
And, seeing this is impossible
in a world so fragmented into sects,
20 where all find grounds for their own straying
in those writings they've set above themselves,   (1331)
I took this other literary road,
which, whether good or not, is dear to me:
to put my own afflictions into verse.

25   Not, as the crowd of mortals may suppose
     (what would be most easy), to gain the empty fruit
     of glory, as they say. Quite the contrary:
     I know that my detractors write in this mode
     rather to display themselves to men: for most of them
30   measure their own measures and those of their fellows;
     nor do I place this over godly labors
     (may God's Word not let such a thing befall me!).
     How I'm minded, then, may well surprise you.
     First, by working for others, I wished
35   so to subdue my own unmeasuredness;   (1332)
     indeed, though I write, I don't write much
     when toiling on the meter. Secondly, for the young,
     especially such as love to read,
     I'd give this as some kind of cheering medicine,
40   guiding the trustful to things most worthy,
     sweetening by artful means the commandments' tartness.
     And the harpstring's tension also likes relaxing,
     if you want this too: if nothing else
     take these in place of songs and lyre tunes.
45   I have given you them for play, if you care to play a bit,
     lest some injury should come to you in your contest for the
         good.
     A third thing I know affects me: not so important a thing,
     perhaps, but it has influenced me: to see to it
     that strangers have no advantage over us in literature.   (1333)
50   For their sake I speak in highly-colored language,
     even though beauty, for us, is in contemplation.
     It's you, the wise, we've played to now.
     Let it be given us to play the lion.
     This fourth I found when stricken with disease,
55   as a consolation: like an aged swan
     to speak to myself with sibilant wings,
     not a dirge, but a song of transition.

Besides these, learn, you wise, our inward things.
If then you are persuaded,
60 it's these words' best use; even those that are in play are words,
so give them room: nothing's too long or overstuffed,
nothing is useless, as I do believe.   (1334)
These very words will teach you, if you're willing.
Some indeed are my own, others from elsewhere:
65 whether a praise of good or blaming of bad men,
or dogmas, or some judgment, or sections of speeches,
kept in the memory by the binding of the letter.
If these things are petty, do grander ones yourself.
You revile meter? No wonder, when you're meterless,
70 an iamb-manufacturer, scribbling abortions.
For who knows what he's witnessed, without seeing?
Or who's raced with a runner, without running?
Or do you forget that, what you blame, you've bought?
For the thing you reproach is what you strive after,
75 being wondrously unmeasured in writing of poems.   (1335)
So what, carping, you fling overboard, faith reels back in,
and the beloved cargo shipwrecks us.
Such things you contrive, you wise.
Aren't they a bald-faced lie, aren't they double?
80 Now an ape to us, and now a lion:
whereby the lust for fame is soon detected.
Know this, too: Scripture is full of meter,
as wise ones of the Hebrew nation say.
Or don't you find meter in the plucking of strings,
85 as men of old sang in well-tuned words,
making a genial vehicle for the good,
informing morals by way of melodies?
Let Saul persuade you of this,
who was freed of a spirit by the harpist's modes.
90 What harm, then, is it to you that the young be led   (1336)
by pleasant solemnities to communion with God?

For they don't bear a change all at once.
For now, let there be some nobler mixture,
and a fixing, when in time the good takes hold,
95 then, drawing away the frills, like scaffolding,
we'll keep that which is good.
What could be more useful?
And don't you add sweet flavors to your meals,
O stern one, with your frowns and scowlings?
100 Why then do you begrudge me my good meter,
judging your neighbor's meters by your own?
Different are the borders of Phrygia and Mysia,
different the flights of eagles and of crows.

Lamentation concerning the Sorrows of His Own Soul

Poem 2.1.45, De animae suae calamitatibus cannen lugubre (PG 37:1353–1378)

Poor soul! What have I suffered! What groan will do
    for me?
What fountain of tears suffice? What melodies?
No one has wept so over his children's death
or that of his kind parents, or cherished wife,   (1354)
5 nor for his sweet homeland, scorched by mordant fire,
nor for his members rotting with hateful sickness,
the way I mourn my soul's dire sufferings,
its heavenly image destroyed (oh misery!).
For truly man is the great God's creature and image,
10 from God proceeding, and to God returning again.
Whoever leans towards what's above, and has tamed the flesh
    by the spirit,
has Christ as his life's merciful guide:
his possession, his tongue and ears, his very mind itself,
and his strength, supplying all things for the life to come,
15 a deliverance from the insatiate world, from all that
Belial, God-hater, thief of other's ownings, has amassed;
but into his barns he brings better stuff than earthly   (1355)
    things,
than things stealable, or corruptible:
to see the Lord himself, and become spirit,

20   and, having laid aside the flesh and the antitype's bulk,
     to gain a standing in the bright angelic choir
     and have a prize surpassing his great struggles,
     seeing no more a vague type of the tabernacle, as formerly,
     nor the law's image, written and undone,
25   but beholding the unchanging one, with a purified
        mind's eye,
     where all mouths celebrate with festal song.
     This is the purpose of human life. To this end, hybris
     scraped up grubbing men for the sufferings of Christ,
     who received the form of a slave, and tasted
30   of death, and obtained another life;
     though God, he lived humbly, he who is eternally from on
        high,
     utterly the eternal image of the deathless Father,   (1356)
     so that he might free me from slavery, from the bonds
        of death,
     and that I might once more attain to a better life.
35   But I, I have not kept God's holy mysteries,
     with a soul initiated in the way again to heaven;
     but the dust's weight weighs me down, nor could I manage
     to cast my gaze to light, when I rose from the mud.
     Yes, cast it! But midway there arose a cloud, blocking the view,
40   the flesh stirred up by a mundane spirit.
     Many cares turn about in my heart, this way and that,
     empty things, from a wandering mind,
     casting Christ, God the Word, far off (for the Bridegroom will
        not
     mingle with a soul that's strange to him);
45   while on the tongue lie many evil poisons of destruction.
     For the tongue is for man a half-part of evil,
     belching out anger, a naked wickedness, which,
        boiling over   (1357)
     ferociously, carries a man out of his mind,

or hides a painful thought within the breast,
50 but speaks smooth talk from a politic mouth.
    O for some door upon my eyes, and for my ears
    that have everywhere been spread abroad, not soundly,
    so that I might see what is good, and receive what's to
        be heard,
    but that both might automatically shut themselves to evils.
55 And the hands' best work is to lift up always to heaven
    holy things, in readiness to practice heaven's laws.
    For the feet, it's to walk a straight road, not on thorns,
    neither along sea-scapes and an unholy path.
    But now, while God provided every member as good, to do
        good things,
60 evil has found them an instrument towards my death.
    What is this law for me? How am I bound upon earth
        by flesh?   (1358)
    How, as a body mingled with light spirit,
    am I not totally mind, a pure nature, nor totally
    a dust of lesser things, but something else, from both, and
        both?
65 Therefore I wage an unending battle of war, with
    flesh and soul opposed to one another.
    I am the image of God, and am drawn to wickedness.
    The worse attacks its better with irreverence.
    Or else I escape wickedness, and stand, not without
        struggling,
70 exercised many ways, with the help of heaven's hand.
    For there is, in me, there is a double law: on the one hand
        there is good,
    which follows what is good; but what is worse
    follows evil things; for, while the mind is ready
    to follow Christ, and will approach the light,
75 the other, of flesh and blood, is eager   (1359)
    to entertain Belial, and be dragged headlong to darkness.

And it delights in material things, things unstable
and fleeting, as if they were good.
It loves carousals, feuds, and fulness of wine,
80 shameful results of shady deeds, and stealth.
It takes the broad way, and delights in self-destruction,
incited by the dismal mists of stupidity.
But the other delights in heavenly things, as though present
already in hope, and it has God alone
85 as life's expectation; things down here it sees as worthless
        smoke,
alien things, subject to alien conditions.
And it loves poverty and sufferings, noble
cares, and travels on the narrow path of life.
And while these strove, observing from above there came
90 the Spirit of the mighty God, and gave the mind a hand, (1360)
ending the pernicious body's warring, and stilling
the rising swell of black passions.
But again, this flesh has a madman's strength, and does
        not let up
warring, but the sword strikes here and there.
95 Sometimes the dust is conquered by the mind; sometimes
        again
the mind unwillingly follows the flesh, as stronger.
While what it wants is what's better, what it hates
it does, bewailing the bitter servitude,
our original father's error, and our mother's lawless
100 persuasion, the mother of our venery,
and the twisted, blood-sucking serpent's shameless lie,
that serpent who delights in humanity's crimes,
and the wood, and the fruit of the plant that crippled
        mankind,
the destroying taste, and the gates of death,

105 an utter shame in nakedness of flesh, and being
  cast out   (1361)
 dishonored from paradise and from the tree of life.
 Sickened with these things, the mind mourns.
  But the flesh
 looks with me now to these first ancestors, and the
  murderous plant,
 and always greets as a most sweet food
110 what the bitter, destroying, cozening snake displays to it.
 So it is that I groan, and in prayers to the Lord
 who rules all things, and holds all in his scales,
 I supplicate concerning soul and body, that he would deign
 to judge between them, and dissipate their warfare,
115 making the worse submit to the better, as is right.
 For this would be far better for them both:
 so that the soul should not drag along the ground, weighed
  down by dust,
 like lead that plummets to the nether depths,
 but that the dust, on wings of spirit, might be raised up (1362)
  also to the image,
120 like some cheap wax devoured by the flame.
 Praying thus, I apply many remedies to the fat flesh,
 and quickly I dispel the noisome sickness.
 Its strength, as of some horrid beast, I check
 with mighty bands, quaking at the evil wave.
125 I set a lock to my stomach, with miserable grief
 I consume my spirit, and shed forth streams of tears.
 I bend worn knees to the Lord, I drag out sleepless nights,
 and am foul, wearing a habit of remorse.
 Banquets, dances, laughter are for others;
130 likewise sprees, the sports of the bright and youthful.
 Others, again, take joy in wives and children,
 and in mighty wealth's soon-to-be-lost acclaim.

Others enjoy their markets and gardens,   (1363)
or baths, and cutting a great figure in the city,
135 being paraded with high-sounding words, while one's
          followers
make a din, and one can be pompous on the high stage.
Yes, many are man's pleasures in this many-sided life;
but happiness has been intermixed with evils.
I, however, have died to this life; I bear but a meager
140 breath upon this earth, and I flee from towns and men.
I hold converse with beasts and rocks, where, alone,
          away from others,
I dwell in a miserable, ramshackle little place.
One coat, no shoes, no hearth, I live on hope
alone, and am a disgrace to all worldly people.
145 My bed is straw, my blankets, reinforced sackcloth;
the dirt floor's dust is watered with tears.
Many are those who groan beneath iron bands;   (1364)
while I've heard that some take ashes for their food;
yet others mix their drink with grievous tears;
150 others, packed about with wintry snow, stand
forty days and nights, like trees,
in their hearts already departed from this earth,
possessing in their minds God only; another has
          clamped shut
his lips, and placed a bridle on his tongue:
155 not always, though, but he takes the bridle off solely
          for hymns,
like a living harp, plucked by the Spirit.
And one devotes his head to Christ; for pure prayer's sake
he keeps it unshorn, a longhair.
Another has closed shut his eyes, and placed doors on
          his ears,
160 lest some deadly spur sneak in, through inattention.
Such is my stock of remedies for the ragings of the dust, (1365)

a helper against my passions, even now when I am gray.
But many storms, unlooked-for, swirl about in spite
    of this,
and wear me out with bitter pains.
165 But it neither yields to words, nor by labors
is it conquered, nor does time tame the horrors.
But always, with blind eyes, it goes boldly
against life, seeking, as they say, the cliffs.
And if even it gives way a little from fear
170 of God, or from pains, or God-given words,
then, like a shoot transplanted by farmers' hands,
it soon is curving back to its former evil.
O members, spawn of death for humankind! Being then
    in this way
consumed by evils, we joy in our insanity.
175 We neither value reason, which God, when granting the
    seed of life,
placed within those who are coming into being,   (1366)
nor do we tremble at the Law, which long ago, in letters
of stone, Christ traced out as the truth,
and the Lord inscribed on a plank, then in our hearts,
180 by the brightness of the good-minded Spirit;
we even plot against Christ's sufferings,
by which he drew me away from bitter passion,
taking flesh, being nailed to the cross, nailing also
the creature's black transgression, and Belial's strength,
185 so that, reborn and racing out of the tomb,
we should have glory anew with the great Christ.
God's gifts are many to all things upon earth,
greater, truly, than our tongue can tell.
And as he subdues my recklessness with his strokes,
    he draws me

190 towards life, supplying things in friendship.
     For he rules all things for men with a kindly mind,   (1367)
     even if the depth of his wisdom is concealed,
     and much fog stands between our race and God,
          which only few
195 have gone through, seeing past our life with most keen eyes,
     and the pure who fasten on to pure wisdom.
     But Christ gave me extraordinary honor:
     first, when he gave my mother a gift, after she had prayed
     from the depths of her heart: she received the gift
200 of offspring, since nothing is better than children among all
          possessions.
     Then later, a divine love of the life of wisdom
     was sent from him by night-time visions.
     Come then, hear now, you of godly minds. But
     profane souls, place doors upon your ears.
205 I was a tender child, not long a child, when the mind
     was etched with an image of good and evil,   (1368)
     not yet having an idea by solid concepts,
     but having at first been inscribed with alien manners.
     But my parents wrote me this mind, not with evil
210 colors, but by teaching the good things of virtue.
     For indeed, they were the wonder of everyone on earth,
     all, at least, who showed the least love of piety.
     Equal alike in age and in renown for the manners
     of human life, happy, healthy
215 beyond measure. He once stood far from the great
          sheepfold,
     where now he greatly governs, not a sheep, since he is
     preferred before the sheep, and over them is shepherd,
     and.is now a father, and a pastor of pastors.
     He did not come into the much-yielding orchard early,   (1369)
220 but, by labor, he outshone those who were before.

And she, the holy fruit of holy parents, from a good
root, and a mother's good branches:
she is not a whit less to be honored than those who earlier
    had received
Christ the Lord, and who saw him reawakened from
    the tomb:
225 though breathing a bit on the ground, by the need of
    the flesh,
they have a greater share of the life above.
From them, my mind new-formed, like a cheese
newly curdled, received at once a molding as from a basket.
And one time, while I slept, there came to me such a dream,
230 one that drew me eagerly to a longing for incorruption.
Two ladies appeared to me in silver garments,
virgins standing side by side, shining,
both beautiful, and of the same age; and for both of them
their make-up was to be without make-up, which is a   (1370)
    woman's beauty.
235 No gold or hyacinth festooned their neck;
they were not dressed in fine-spun silken fabric,
nor, again, enveloped in coats of soft linen;
nor was their eye done up with penciled eyelids;
nor had they so many curiously-wrought potions of lechery,
240 to madden men with their feminine looks;
nor did blond hair in braids flow down their backs,
stirred all the while with the breath of temperate winds.
But a beautiful mantle they wore, tied with a belt,
from the bones of the neck right down to their feet;
245 and above, their head and cheeks were covered
by a veil, while they fixed their eyes on the ground.
The fair blush of shame was prominent in both,
as much as would show from behind the well-spun cloak.
And the lips of each lay closed in silence,   (1371)

250 like a rose in its bedewed calyx.
Seeing them, I was greatly happy. For I thought
they were greater than mortals, and that not a little.
And with their lips, again, they kissed me, since their spirit
        was cheered,
cherishing me as a beloved son.
255 And when I asked the women who and whence they were,
"Chastity," said one; the other, "Temperance":
"We stand alongside Christ the King,
rejoicing in the beauties of the virgin ones of heaven.
But come now, child, mix your mind with our mind,
260 and your torch with our torches,
so that we may carry you up on high through the bright,
        shining air,
and set you as a light beside the immortal Trinity."
So saying, they took off through the air. But my eye   (1372)
followed them as they flew away. And so it was, they
        were a dream;
265 but a long while my heart rejoiced in the holy visions of the
        night,
with these images of shining incorruption.
Even now the story comes to mind, since the notion
of good and evil was fixed infallibly.
And a sense of longing leads the way, and the obscure
        beauty
270 of a late night hour is clearly visible.
And just as a hidden spark, consuming from within
a dried-up stalk, lights it up suddenly—
first a tiny flame, then afterward springs up
unspeakable fire—so I too, kindled by the apparition,
275 swiftly am ignited in love, and the blaze is visible to all,
no longer hidden away in the depths of the soul.

So first, I sought the company of holy people, who
    had shed   (1373)
the bonds of wedlock, and were freed from this earthly
    world,
so that together they might fly in pursuit of Christ the King,
280 leaving this life with plenteous glory.
And, as I both loved and frequented them with all my heart,
I had them as guides of the hope of heaven;
but later, I set aside the heavy yoke of marriage,
desiring the high prize of those who are ever in bloom.
285 For indeed, all the unwedded natures who have received
the wide heaven as their lot are superior to vexing passions.
Incomparably dazzling is the great God; and like God
are the servants who stand near him who is throned on high,
bearing the first ray of light from the pure God—
290 all-luminous, bestowing lights to mortals.   (1374)
But those that are gathered in one from soul and body
and are double, the offspring of belligerent dust,
these desire wedlock and are eager to sow
upon bodies. But the Word, possessing a better inheritance,
295 set it far from the flesh, and kept it apart from the world's
    delusion,
but placed it nearby the unfettered life of immortals.
Desire set me going after this in a big way; I would not
plant a feeble footstep on the soil.
But as one that had tasted the sweet milk and honey
300 of the firm and lasting choir that is there,
I did not want to be followed near by the bitter food
of soul-devouring evil inwardly gnawing.
Not for me parties and suchlike things that preoccupy
    youth,   (1375)
no designer clothes or luxuriant hair,
305 nor the ungifted gift of scurrilous talk, nor unchecked
laughter, the favorite convulsions

of the foul-minded flesh. Hills, boundaries, neighing
horses and the noise of hunting dogs
I have left for others; shaking off all finery
310 I have set my neck under stem Discretion,
who preserved me and loved me and raised me to high honor,
and readily set me into the hands of Christ.
But, O Father, O Word of the Father, and you, O shining Spirit,
the support of our life that is in a bad way,
315 do not leave me to the meddlesome hands of the
enemy, the antagonist against your hope;
lest I be like a ship, tarred, trim sailing, running straight,
even already pressing close to shore—
a hurricane of fearsome winds, which falls on a sudden,   (1376)
320 mocks it, and would send it straight
back again upon the open sea of life,
tossed about here and there by mighty evils,
and would dash it upon the unseen rocks.
For such is the mind of Belial, full of envy;
325 he ever hates the race of men; he does not want them
dwelling away from earth in heaven, since he himself
was shaken from heaven to this ground, for his conniving,
the ill-fated one, who longed to have the acclaim
of the original light, and the great, royal honor of God;
330 instead of lights, he has been clothed with hateful darkness.
Because of this, works of darkness always cheer him,
and he takes strength where there is shady vice.
Moreover, he is wholly double of form, and twisted in thought,
corning up now with one trap, now another.
335 Now, to be sure, he is absolute darkness; but if you   (1377)
        should find him,
he is swiftly transformed into an angel of light.
And while he softly laughs, he deceives the mind. Therefore, be
        extremely
wise, lest, in place of lights, you come to death.

For even a worse man knows he should flee from evil;
340 for obvious evil is hateful to many.
But I praise the one who convicts what lurks invisible,
seeing with most penetrating eyes of the spirit.
But save my old, gray head,
and grant a merciful end to life, as formerly
345 you carefully loved me, and day by day you led me to
what's best, bringing me forward to better hopes;
and lead me away from ill-willed, bitter cares
into the fair haven of your kingdom;
so that, while extolling you with the ever-living lights,   (1378)
350 I may have a portion of heavenly glory, O Lord.

To His Own Soul

Poem 2.1.78, Ad suam animam (PG 37:1425–1426).

You have a job to do, soul, and a great one, if you like:
examine yourself, what it is you are and how you act,
where you come from, and where you're going to end,
and whether to live is this very life you're living, or something
    else besides.
5 You have a job to do, soul; by these things cleanse your life.
Make me to know God and God's mysteries.
What was there before this universe, and why is this universe
    here for you?
Where has it come from, and where is it going?
You have a job to do, soul, by these things cleanse your life.
10 How does God guide and turn the universe:
or why are some things permanent, while other things
    flow away,   (1426)
and us especially, in this changing life?
You have a job to do, soul: look to God alone.
What was my former glory, what is this present arrogance?
15 What will be my crown, and what the end of my life?
Of these things inform me, and check the mind from
    wandering.
A job you have to do, soul: lest you suffer in deep trouble.

Epitaph on St Basil

(Epitaph 119, PG 38:72)

I had thought that a body could as well
live without a soul
as me without you,
Basil, beloved servant of Christ;
but you're gone and I remain.
What'll become of us?
Will you not set me, when I arise,
there with you in the choir of the blessed?
No, don't leave me: I swear by my grave
I won't leave yours, not willingly.
You have Gregory's word.

Select Bibliography

1. Texts and translations

McGuckin, John, trans., *Saint Gregory Nazianzen: Selected Poems* (Fairacres, Oxford: Sisters of the Love of God Press, 1986).

Meehan, Dennis Molaise, trans., *Saint Gregory of Nazianzus. Three Poems: Concerning His Own Affairs, Concerning Himself and the Bishops, Concerning His Own life,* Fathers of the Church 75 (Washington, D.C.: Catholic University of America Press, 1987).

Moreschini, Claudio, ed., D. A. Sykes, trans. and commentary, *St Gregory of Nazianzus: Poemata Arcana* (Oxford: Clarendon Press, 1997).

Moreschini, Claudio, et al., eds., *Gregorio Nazianzeno: Poesie,* 1 (Roma: Citta Nuova Editrice, 1994).

Norris, Frederick W., Lionel Wickham, and Frederick Williams, *Faith Gives Fullness to Reasoning: The Five Theological Orations of Gregory Nazianzen,* Suppl. to VigCh, XIII (Leiden: E. J. Brill, 1991).

Schaff, Philip, and Henry Wace, eds., *S. Cyril of Jerusalem; S. Gregory Nazianzen,* Nicene and Post-Nicene Fathers, second series, vol. 7 (Grand Rapids, MI: Wm. B. Eerdmans Publishing Co., reprinted 1983). (Nazianzen section translated and edited by Charles Gordon Browne and James Edward Swallow.)

Werhahn, Heinz Martin, ed., *Gregorii Nazianzeni Σύγκισις βίων,* Klassisch-Philologische Studien 15 (Wiesbaden: Otto Harrassowitz, 1953).

White, Carolinne, *Gregory of Nazianzus: Autobiographical Poems,* Cambridge Medieval Classics 6 (Cambridge: Cambridge University Press, 1996).

Wyss, Bernhard. "Zu Gregor von Nazianz," in *Phyllobolia, für P. von der Mühll* (Basel 1946), 153–183. [Contains text of 60 extra lines in poem 1.1.9.]

2. Studies

Ackermann, Walter, *Die didaktische Poesie des Gregorius von Nazianz* (Leipzig, 1903).

Gallay, Paul, *La vie de saint Grégoire de Nazianze* (Lyon/Paris, 1943).

Gilbert, Peter, "Person and Nature in the Theological Poems of St Gregory of Nazianzus" (Ph.D. diss., Catholic University of America, Washington, D.C., 1995).

Meredith, Anthony, *The Cappadocians* (Crestwood, NY: St Vladimir's Seminary Press, 1995).

Milovanovic-Barham, Celica. "Gregory of Nazianzus: Ars Poetica (In suos versus: Carmen 2.1.39)," *Journal of Early Christian Studies* 5.4 (1997): 497–510.

Misch, Georg, *A History of Autobiography in Antiquity* (Cambridge, MA: 1951).

Musurillo, H., "The Poetry of Gregory of Nazianzus," *Thought* 45 (1970): 45–55.

Norris, Frederick, "Gregory of Nazianzen's Doctrine of Jesus Christ" (Ph.D. diss., Yale University, New Haven, 1970).

———, "Of Thorns and Roses: The Logic of Belief in Gregory Nazianzen," *Church History* 53 (1984): 455–64.

Otis, Brooks, "Cappadocian Thought as a Coherent System," *Dumbarton Oaks Papers* 12 (1958), 95–124.

———, "The Throne and the Mountain: An Essay on Gregory Nazianzus," *The Classical Journal* 56 (1961): 146–65.

Patterson, Lloyd G, "Nikaia to Constantinople: The Theological Issues," *Greek Orthodox Theological Review* 27 (1982): 375–93.

Pelikan, Jaroslav, *Christianity and Classical Culture: The Metamorphosis of Natural Theology in the Christian Encounter with Hellenism* (New Haven and London, 1993).

Pellegrino, Michele, *La Poesia di S. Gregorio Nazianzeno* (Milan, 1932).

Plagnieux, Jean, *Saint Grégoire de Nazianze Théologien,* Études de Science Religieuse 7 (Paris, 1951).

Rapisarda, E., "Il pessimismo di Gregorio Nazianzeno," *Studi bizantini e neoellenici* 7 (1953): 189–201.

Ritter, A. M., *Das Konzil von Konstantinopel und sein Symbol* (Gottingen, 1965).

Rousseau, Philip, *Basil of Caesarea* (Berkeley and Los Angeles, 1994).

Ruether, Rosemary Radford, *Gregory of Nazianzus, Rhetor and Philosopher* (Oxford, 1969).

Spidlik, T., *Grégoire de Nazianze: Introduction à l'étude de sa doctrine spirituelle* (Rome, 1971).

Sykes, D. A. "The Poemata Arcana of St Gregory Nazianzen," *Journal of Theological Studies* n.s. 21 (1970): 32–42.

_____, "The Poemata Arcana of St Gregory Nazianzen: Some Literary Questions," *Byzantinische Zeitschrift* 72 (1979): 6–15.

_____, "Understandings of the Church in the Cappadocians," in H. Davies, ed., *Studies of the Church in History* (Pittsburgh, 1983), 73–83.

_____, "Gregory Nazianzen as didactic poet," *Studia Patristica* 16.2 (1985): 433–37.

_____, "Gregory Nazianzen, poet of the moral life," *Studia Patristica* 22 (1989): 69–73.

Trypanis, Constantine, *Greek Poetry from Homer to Seferis* (Chicago, 1981).

Wesche, Kenneth Paul, "The Union of God and man in Jesus Christ in the Thought of Gregory of Nazianzus," *St Vladimir's Theological Quarterly,* 28 (1984): 83–98.

Wilson, Anna M., "Reason and Revelation in the Conversion Accounts of the Cappadocians and Augustine," in B. Bruning, et al., eds., *Collectanea Augustiniana* 1 (Leuven, 1990), 259–78.

Winslow, Donald F., *The Dynamics of Salvation: A Study in Gregory of Nazianzus,* Patristic Monograph Series 7 (Cambridge, MA, 1979).

Wyss, Bernhard, *Gregor von Nazianz: ein griechisch-christlicher Dichter des vierten Jahrhunderts* (Darmstadt, 1962, reprint).

POPULAR PATRISTICS SERIES

ST VLADIMIR'S SEMINARY PRESS
1-800-204-2665 • www.svspress.com